# A SHORT HISTORY
# OF WESTERN ATHEISM

# A Short History of Western Atheism

JAMES THROWER

Distributed by

**ℝ** *Prometheus Books*

an ethical humanist press

923 Kensington Ave.
Buffalo, New York 14215

PEMBERTON BOOKS

First published 1971 by Pemberton Books
(Pemberton Publishing Co Ltd), 88 Islington
High Street, London N1 8 EN

© 1971 James Thrower

SBN 0 301 71101 1 *cloth*
     0 301 71102 X *paper*

Printed in Great Britain by
Richard Clay (The Chaucer Press) Ltd,
Bungay, Suffolk

TO MY MOTHER AND
THE MEMORY OF MY FATHER

# ACKNOWLEDGMENTS

I SHOULD LIKE TO THANK the University of Ghana and especially my old Head of Department, Professor Christian Baeta, for allowing me a term's study-leave in 1968 to begin work on this book. Mr Andrew Walls of the Department of Religious Studies, Mr Nigel Dower of the Department of Logic and Moral Philosophy, and Dr George Molland of the Department of History and Philosophy of Science—colleagues in the University of Aberdeen—were kind enough to read the proofs. Miss Amelia Davidson of Robert Gordon's College, Aberdeen, prepared the Index. I would like to thank all those without whose labours this book would not have been possible, and whom, I trust, I have duly acknowledged both in the text and in the footnotes—not least the *atheoi* themselves, and were it not for the greater debt acknowledged in the dedication this short work would surely have been dedicated to them.

*James Thrower*
*June 1971*

# CONTENTS

# INTRODUCTION

IT WAS COMMON PRACTICE until quite recently for apologetic theologians to begin their discussion of the evidence for a religious, and more particularly, a theistic world view with reference to what is known as the *argumentum e consensu gentium*, the argument from the general consent of mankind. It is an extremely venerable argument. Lactantius, writing in the third century AD, appealed to it when he spoke of 'the consideration that has for its support the testimony of peoples and nations that differ not in this one particular'.[1] Plato, some six centuries previously, had also appealed to the fact, as he took it to be, that 'all mankind, Greeks and non-Greeks alike, believe in the existence of gods'.[2] More recently, Professor John Baillie evokes it as the first argument of his theistic apologia, stating quite categorically 'that we know of no human society, however savage and backward, which does not already find itself confronted by the divine'.[3] That such a consensus existed has not always been agreed—it was particularly doubted, for instance, in the eighteenth century—but from the historical and anthropological evidence now available it would appear reasonably certain that what may be loosely termed religious belief has in the past been the norm rather than the exception among the peoples of the world.

This situation has now changed, at least within what is known as Western European culture. Dr C. S. Lewis, in his inaugural lecture to the chair of Mediaeval and Renaissance Literature at the University of Cambridge in 1951, placed a divide between our own age, which he took as beginning towards the end of the last century, and all that preceded it, primarily in terms of past acceptance and present rejection of a supernatural picture of the world.[4] In the light of this divide, he said, older divisions of cultural history, such as those dividing Classical Antiquity from the Dark Ages, and the latter from the Middle Ages and the Renaissance faded into insignificance. What we are witnessing and living through today is the transition from a theistically and supernaturally orientated culture to one orientated naturalistically, something which Lewis saw to be fraught with the most serious consequences for all aspects of our life. Put positively, we are witnessing today the rise of a secularism more widespread and pervasive than has ever existed before and Lewis makes the important point that this secularism is to be distinguished, not only from the ages of Faith, but also from Paganism with which it is often confused. 'A post-Christian man,' he says, 'is not a Pagan; you might as well think that a married woman recovers her virginity by divorce. The post-Christian is cut off from the Christian past and doubly from the Pagan past.'[5] His point here is the same as that made by Canon Demant when he says 'that the ancient paganisms, the Bible and the Christian Church all have this in common, that they hold the source of all things to be a divine reality which transcends the world as well as operating within it. The secularisms of today have this in common that they hold the meaning of the world to lie within itself.'[6]

But while the situation today is to a large extent unique, particularly in its extent, it is not wholly without precedent and the origins of this situation go back at least as far as the latter part of the Renaissance and, as I hope to show, even further. Which brings me to my theme.

While it is true that in the past and until quite recently—'the day before yesterday' as Lewis puts it—our common frame of reference was a religious or supernatural interpretation of the world, it must not be overlooked that there has existed at certain periods of our intellectual and cultural history a small number of thinkers and schools who have consciously rejected such an interpretation and held as an alternative, in some form or other, a naturalistic view of the world. It is this, the so far neglected and well-nigh unrecorded history of unbelief that I wish to look at in the pages which follow. My plan will be to note those thinkers and schools which have been or which might be called agnostic or atheistic, beginning with the roots of the Western intellectual tradition as these are found in Greece and Rome and to a lesser extent, so far as concerns religious unbelief, in Israel. The significant period for the rise of the secularist attitude in Western Europe is, I think, the late Middle Ages and the dissociation of faith and reason—or, as I shall express it, the limitation placed upon the scope of reason—which then took place, and which gave rise to the development of physical science as an exclusive and exhaustive way of looking at the world.

It will also be part of my purpose to try to isolate the mainsprings of atheism and to try to show what are the leading issues which divide the believer from the unbeliever, the theist from the agnostic and the atheist. My purpose, therefore, is not simply that of a historian of ideas, for I hope to shed some philosophical light on what is one of the dominating discussions of our time. There is about atheism an organic character, and I would therefore disagree with the judgment of Charles B. Upton, who, writing on the subject of 'Atheism' in the *Encyclopaedia of Religion and Ethics*, says that 'the history of it is little more than a collection of instances in which doubt and negation in regard to some essential element in theism have arisen'.[7] There is more to atheism than this. The naturalistic outlook has a consistency which makes it a genuine and alternative way of looking at the world from that which has inspired the religious believer. In one sense, of course, Upton is right. Much atheism, as we shall see, can be understood only in the light of the current theism which it was concerned to reject. Such atheism is relative. There is, however, a way of looking at and interpreting events in the world, whose origins, as I shall hope to show, can be seen as early as the beginnings of speculative thought itself, and which I shall call naturalistic, that is atheistic *per se*, in the sense that it is incompatible with any and every form of supernaturalism. While we shall note the relative atheisms it will be obvious that naturalistic or absolute atheism is both fundamentally more important, and more interesting, representing as it does one polarity in the development of the human spirit, and it is on this that I shall concentrate in the pages which follow.

NOTES

[1] Lactantius, *Institutorum*. Lib. I. *De Falsa Religione* § 2

[2] Plato, *Laws*, 886a

[3] J. Baillie, *Our Knowledge of God* p 6

[4] C. S. Lewis, *De Descriptione Temporum*. Reprinted in his book, *They Asked for a Paper*.

[5] *They Asked for a Paper* p 20

[6] V. A. Demant, *Religion and The Decline of Capitalism* p 111

[7] *Encyclopaedia of Religion and Ethics* (Ed Hastings) Vol 1. Article, 'Atheism' p 174

# PART I

# ATHEISM IN CLASSICAL ANTIQUITY

# ONE

# THE PRE-SOCRATIC PERIOD

MANY OF THE ISSUES involved in the dialogue of religion with atheism are as old as thought itself and our study therefore begins where European speculation began; with that awakening of the philosophical spirit among the Ionian physical philosophers during the early part of the sixth century before Christ. This philosophy is called Ionian because it was begun by Thales and his successors Anaximander and Anaximenes at Miletus, one of the Greek colonies on the coast of Asia Minor. For this reason they are also sometimes referred to as the Milesian philosophers. They are termed 'physical philosophers' because their primary concern was with the nature of what they called 'becoming'—that is, with the way in which the world works, though they were also led from this to ask further questions about the world's ultimate origin, and to the postulation of some primary substance out of which the plurality of things which we now observe in the world came. Their inquiries culminated two centuries later in the atomistic theories of Leucippus and Democritus.

But these early philosophers, or scientists as some would call them, do not come before us like Melchisedek, without genealogy. That great student of Ancient Greece, F. M. Cornford, warns us in one of his works against those who would write the history of Greek philosophy as if Thales 'had suddenly dropped from the sky and as he bumped the earth ejaculated; "everything must be made of water"'.[1] The Milesian thinkers have an ancestry and to truly understand their originality it will be necessary to look briefly into this for it in no way detracts from the very real and fruitful innovations which are associated with their names and which are directly relevant to our theme. Quite the contrary in fact is seen to be the case when we compare their way of understanding the natural world with that which existed before their time, and in breaking away from which lies their true originality.

But before looking at the differences which divide the new species of philosophers from the old mythological writers let us look at some of the general influences which contributed to the Milesian approach. Among these must be accounted the debt which they owed to the Egyptians and the Babylonians, the Theogonic writings of Hesiod, and perhaps as, if not more important than these, the spirit of the age and the cultural background of the time and place in which they lived. Professor W. K. C. Guthrie, in the first volume of his monumental *History of Greek Philosophy*, writing of this background, calls our attention to the important economic position of Miletus and the high standard of living which it afforded. He describes its culture as one which 'may be broadly described as humanistic and materialistic in tendency', and he continues: 'Its high standard of living was too obviously the product of human energy, resource and initiative for it to acknowledge any great debt to the gods. The poetry of the Ionian Mimnermus was an appropriate expression of its spirit in the late seventh century. To him it seemed that, if there were gods, they must have more sense than to trouble their heads about human affairs. "From the gods we know neither good nor evil." The poet looked inward, at human life itself. He extolled the enjoyment of momentary pleasures and the gathering of roses while they lasted, mourned the swift passing of youth and the misery and feebleness of old age. The philosopher of the same period and society looked outward to the world of nature, and matched his human wits against its secrets. Both are intelligible products of the same material culture, and the same secular spirit.'[2]

Further, the influence exercised by the partial rationalization of the myths of the traditional religion, begun by the writers of the Theogonies, chief among whom was Hesiod, is for some scholars an important transitional stage between the older mythological writers, such as Homer, and the new philosophers. To the relationship, therefore, between the traditional religion and the new philosophy we now turn.

Philosophy began, according to Guthrie, when 'the conviction began to take shape in men's minds that the apparent chaos of events must conceal underlying order, and that this order is the product of impersonal forces',[3] thus giving rise to a form of explanation of events in the world in sharp contrast to that offered by the traditional polytheistic religion, which may be called mythological. This latter type of explanation is nowhere better described than in the opening sections of Professor G. Lowes Dickinson's book *The Greek View of Life*. As he there points out, the gods of the traditional Greek pantheon acted as an explanation both of events in nature and of those human passions and actions which could not be ascribed to human intent. He cites a number of passages from that Bible of Greek culture, the Homeric corpus, in illustration of this point, and it will be as well for us to look at at least one of them in detail, for the issue which the Milesian philosophers raise in rejecting such an explanation is basic to the debate between belief and unbelief both in their day and ours. It is one which we shall see recurring throughout the Western intellectual tradition.

I shall take Professor Lowes Dickinson's first example. He takes it from Homer's *Odyssey*. Odysseus is on his way back to Ithaca from Troy sailing on the 'wine dark sea' when a sudden storm arises. The Homeric explanation for this occurrence is as follows: 'Now the Lord, the shaker of the earth, on his way from the Ethiopians, espied Odysseus afar off from the mountains of the Solymi: even thence he saw him as he sailed over the deep; and he was yet more angered in spirit, and wagging his head he communed with his own heart. "Lo now, it must be that the gods have at the last changed their purpose concerning Odysseus, while I was away among the Ethiopians. And now he is nigh to the Phaeacian land, where it is so ordained that he escape the great issues of the woe which hath come upon him. But methinks, that even yet I will drive him far enough in the path of suffering."'

'With that he gathered the clouds and troubled the waters of the deep, grasping his trident in his hands; and he roused all storms of all manners of winds, and shrouded in clouds the land and sea: and down sped night from heaven. The East Wind and the South Wind clashed, and the stormy West and the North, that is born in the bright air, rolling onward a great wave.'[4]

Those more familiar with the Hebrew Bible will be able to compare this passage from the Homeric corpus with any number of similar, if more impressively and soberly written, accounts of the doings of the god, Yahweh, as recounted in that work.

Events in the world, mythology says, occur as the result of the activity of higher wills and are the result of personal forces pitted against, though sometimes also favourable, to our own. So also with human passions which often come upon us and appear to possess us not by, but against our will. Here too the mythological writers had a ready explanation in terms of conscious and alien wills. An onslaught of love was the work of Aphrodite, musical and artistic inspiration of Apollo, wisdom in a man was the gift of Athene and folly occurred because Zeus had taken away a man's wits.

The breaking away from this way of interpreting events in the world, so far at least as physical phenomena were concerned, and the offering in its place an explanation in terms of necessity, constitutes the real innovation of the Ionian philosophers and allows us to regard them as the first representatives of that understanding of the world upon which, when fully developed, our contemporary culture rests. As Guthrie puts it: 'Under the influence of the earliest philosophical thinking, the "Father of gods and men" and his divine family were dissolved into an impersonal "necessity", an affair of natural laws and the interaction of "airs, ethers, waters and other strange things", as Socrates calls them in the *Phaedo*.'[5]

That this was a new beginning was recognized as early as the fifth century by Aristotle, to whom we owe the distinction between those who described the world in terms of myth and the supernatural and those who first attempted to account for it by means of natural forces. The former he termed the 'theologi' and the latter the 'physiologi', and he ascribed the new beginning to Thales of Miletus.[6]

But although this was a new beginning, Frankfort's remark, that the early philosophers proceeded 'with a preposterous boldness on an entirely unproved assumption'[7] would seem a little extreme. The Milesian thinkers were familiar as we know with the mathematics of the Egyptians and the Babylonians and with the use to which the latter put their knowledge in predicting the movements of the heavenly bodies—at that time regarded by the Greeks as divine persons. Indeed tradition records that Thales successfully used this acquired knowledge to predict the eclipse of 585 BC. It is not, therefore, beyond the bounds of possibility that the first inklings that the world was governed by law, and not by divine caprice, as it was in Homer, was not 'an unproved assumption' but one that could have been deduced from the successful predictions of their Babylonian predecessors, which may well have led them to doubt the divinity of natural forces.

Mythological explanation had not only sought to account for day to day events in the world, but had also tried to satisfy curiosity with regard to the world's far off origin. Hesiod's *Theogony* in particular had offered a mythological account of the generation of the world from the divine ancestors Earth and Heaven, and this, especially with reference to the form in which it was written, no doubt also helped, as we suggested earlier, to pave the way for Ionian speculation on this problem. Whether Hesiod himself had got to the stage of regarding his gods as the personification of natural forces is something about which we cannot be certain, but by the time we come to the Ionian thinkers few traces of the mythological approach remain. Their approach consists, as Guthrie puts it, 'in the abandonment, at all levels of conscious thought, of mythological solutions to problems concerning the origin and nature of the universe and the processes that go on within it. For religious faith there is substituted the faith that was and remains the basis of scientific thought with all its triumphs and with all its limitations: that is, the faith that the visible world conceals a rationality and intelligible order, that the causes of the natural world are to be sought within its boundaries, and that autonomous reason is our sole and sufficient instrument for the search.'[8]

This opinion, to the effect that we have here at the very outset of Greek, and therefore of European thought, the beginnings of that purely secular approach to the world with which we today are so familiar is the opinion not only of Guthrie, whom we have just quoted, but of many other classical scholars as well.

John Burnet, some half-century ago, thought likewise and his work on this period—*The Early Greek Philosophers*—is still regarded as a standard one by many contemporary scholars. In this book Burnet maintained not only that Ionian science, as he called it, was an indigenous outcrop, owing nothing to either the traditional religion or to the superimposed Achaian beliefs, a view we have seen reason to qualify, but he also asserts roundly the secular and naturalistic character of Ionian speculation. That the Milesians continued to employ the word 'god' or 'the divine' in their talk about nature was not taken by Burnet to have any religious significance whatever. 'We must not be misled,' he writes, 'by the use of the word "theos" in the remains that have come down to us. It is quite true that the Ionians applied it to the "primary substance" and to the world or worlds, but this means no more and no less than the use of divine epithets "ageless" and "deathless". . . . In its religious sense the word "god" always means first and foremost an object of worship, but already in Homer that had ceased to be its only signification. Hesiod's *Theogony* is the best evidence of the change. It is clear that many of the gods mentioned were never worshipped by any-one and some of them are mere personifications of human passions. This non-religious use of the word "god" is charac-teristic of the whole period . . . and it is of the first importance to realize it. No one who does so will fall into the error of deriving science from mythology.'[9]

This would appear to me to be far too extreme and I think it might be questioned, as indeed it has been, whether Ionian thinking was, in its initial phase, as extremely and overtly secular and naturalistic as Burnet and, to a lesser extent Guthrie, have maintained. That the Milesian philosophers broke with the older mythological explanation of events in the world as the outcome of divine caprice cannot be doubted but what can and has been doubted is whether we have in them a com-pletely secular approach which would entirely deny the reality of the Divine, as that upon which the world rests and by which it is ordered. It is not certain that they took a naturalistic understanding of the process of 'becoming' as exhausting their understanding of the world and that in their ontology—that is their view of what there is—only impersonal natural forces had a place. Werner Jaeger, in his Gifford Lectures entitled *The Theology of the Early Greek Philosophers* thinks not, and he accuses Burnet, as he would I feel have accused Guthrie had his work been available when he wrote, of reading back into the sixth century Ionians the mind of a late nineteenth century physicist.[10] His own reading of the Ionians is so far removed from this 'positivistic' interpretation, as he calls it, that he not only denies the naturalistic interpretation *in toto*, but sees both Thales and Anaximander not as atheists but, in one side of their work at least, as offering us a new and an extremely sophisticated metaphysical conception of the divine. He goes even further and claims for Anaximander the title of the first natural theologian and in support of his case refers us to Anaximander's substantive use of the term 'apeiron'—the Unlimited or the Boundless—which for him was the primal principle or 'arche' —and to the predicates with which he describes it; 'unborn', 'imperishable', 'all-encompassing' and 'all-governing' and then invites us to concur with Aristotle in the judgment that for Anaximander, this is the divine. So also, with regard to Thales' dictum that 'all things are full of gods'. Jaeger's opinion is that while the word 'god' is being used by Thales somewhat differently from the way in which it was used in the traditional religion, it is still being used in a religious sense. What Thales is saying, according to Jaeger, is that new experience of nature provides us with a new source of knowledge of the divine.

Much, if not everything, here depends upon how much or how little we read into the predicate 'divine'. Guthrie, like Burnet, tends to dismiss the use of this term without much ado. Writing of Thales' use of the term as a predicate of his primal substance, water, he takes him as meaning that water must contain within itself the cause of motion and change, and to the Greek, this would mean, he says, that it must be of the nature of 'psyche', life or soul-stuff, and therefore alive and everlasting. 'At this point,' he writes, 'the Greek mind goes a step further. Ask any Greek what, if anything, in his experience is ever-living . . . and he would have only one answer: *theos* or *to theion*. Everlasting life is the mark of the divine and of nothing else. Hence, Thales, though rejecting the anthropomorphic deities of popular religion, could retain its language to the extent of saying that in a special sense, the whole world was filled with gods. One may compare the use of the divine attributes in Anaximander.'[11] Professor A. H. Armstrong takes a similar line when he writes that 'this stuff they called divine, by which they probably meant no more than that it is living and everlasting'.[12]

Jaeger's understanding of the usage of *to theion* goes beyond this and he sees a very definitive motive in the retention of this concept in both Thales and Anaximander. 'What happens in Anaximander's argument' he writes, '(and that of his successors in this line) is that the predicate God, or rather the Divine is transferred from the traditional deities to the first principle of Being (at which they arrived by rational investigation) on the ground that the predicates usually attributed to the gods of Homer and Hesiod are inherent in that principle to a higher degree or can be assigned to it with a greater certainty.'[13]

He then proceeds to detail the subsequent developments of this novel suggestion, especially in Anaxagoras and to a greater extent in post-Socratic philosophy.

Thus if Jaeger is right, far from being naturalists, in the atheistical sense of that term, the Milesian philosophers laid the foundations for that metaphysical conception of the Godhead which the Greek Fathers of the Christian church were to bring to fruition some eight and nine centuries later. His final conclusion is that 'in this so-called natural philosophy we have found theology, theogony, and theodicy functioning side by side. . . . The development of the idea of *kosmos* means both a new way of looking upon the organization of the state as derived from the eternal laws of Being, and a re-creation of religion in terms of the idea of God and the divine government of the world as revealed in nature. That this is not peculiar to Anaximander but remains intrinsically bound up with the new philosophical approach, is clear from the way it recurs in Anaximenes.'[14]

Etienne Gilson, in the first chapter of his book, *God and Philosophy*, also attacks the naturalistic interpretation of the

Ionian philosophers. Referring to the passage which we have quoted from Burnet, Gilson writes, 'My only objection is that very few words have a more distinctly religious connotation than the word "god" . . . every one is entitled to interpret the sentence "all things are full of gods" as meaning that there is not a single god in anything, but the least that can be said of it is that it is a rather bold interpretation.'[15]

R. G. Collingwood comes to a similar conclusion in his study of the Greek, which he contrasts with Renaissance and modern, philosophies of nature. For Collingwood, Ionian, no less than the rest of the Greek approaches to nature is distinguished by the presupposition that the world of nature is saturated and permeated by mind. The world of nature, he says, is for the Greek not only alive, but intelligent, and he comments very significantly: 'Greek thinkers regarded the presence of mind in nature as the source of that regularity and orderliness in the natural world whose presence made a science of nature possible.'[16] Collingwood holds that the mechanical view of nature (Guthrie's 'impersonal forces') does not arise until the latter part of the Renaissance. The Greek view by contrast he describes as organic.

Our conclusion must therefore be, I think, that if we look to the Ionian philosophers for a wholly naturalistic interpretation of the world then we look in vain. Not only do they regard nature as living and therefore divine, but as Jaeger shows, there lies in their thinking at least the germ of the subsequent development of a metaphysical conception of God. But having recognized this, what is also true, and must from our point of view be emphasized, is that in their approach to nature and the origin of the world there lies also the beginnings of the naturalistic position which other thinkers, particularly the Atomists in the next century, will take up and bring to explicit articulation. This, and this is a point of some significance for the debate between belief and unbelief, lies more perhaps in the limited range of their questions—or at least in the limited range that others saw in their questions—than in anything else; something that Aristotle saw when he chided them with having an interest in material causes only rather than in ultimate ones.

Their place in the history of unbelief is therefore ambiguous. What is certainly true is that they laid the foundations for the decline of the old mythological conception of the gods and of traditional religion—though this, of course, only at the intellectual level. But as A. N. Whitehead once remarked, 'The progress of religion is defined by the denunciation of gods',[17] and in the light of what we have said this would appear to be as true of the Ionians as we shall see that it is of the majority of thinkers in the Greek tradition; for we shall, in fact, come across very few examples of absolute atheism. The majority of thinkers whom later writers designated *atheoi* are found upon closer examination to deny only the notion of the gods as expressed in popular belief, and this more often than not as a prelude to the putting forward of a more sophisticated and developed conception of the divine. For this kind of denial Max Müller has suggested that the term 'adevism' is a more accurate description than atheism and he is surely right.[18]

Such a word aptly describes the Ionians, for if they are the first natural philosophers, they are also the first natural theologians as well. It was perhaps something of an injustice to them that the purely naturalistic side of their thinking should subsequently have exercised the greatest influence, for this side of their understanding of the world was seized upon by the Atomists and by others also in the next century and used as a weapon, not only against the mythological approach to phenomena, but against any living conception of the divine. It was for this reason that Plato regarded the development of their approach as a spiritual peril and brought to opposing it all the powers of his mind.

But before we come to look at this highly significant period there are other figures in the Pre-Socratic tradition who merit some consideration in the light of judgments made upon them by later generations.

Drachmann, in his study of *Atheism in Pagan Antiquity*, gives a list of those Greek philosophers whom later generations designated *atheoi* or accused of impiety.[19] In the period before Socrates these included Xenophanes and Anaxagoras, who were accused of impiety; Diogenes of Apollonia, Hippo of Rhegium, Protagoras, Prodicus, Critias and Diagoras of Melos who were all accused of atheism. Let us look now at these and at some of the other figures in the Pre-Socratic period whom, while they are not mentioned by Drachmann, certainly call for our attention.

Xenophanes is certainly not an atheist but an adevist, and in the period before Plato he is perhaps our most certain and best example of such. He is best known for attacking current anthropomorphic conceptions of the gods in a satirical but serious way. His best sayings are worth quoting: 'Men believe that the gods,' he is reported as saying, 'are clothed and shaped and speak like themselves.'[20] And more bitingly, 'If oxen and horses and lions could draw and paint, they would delineate their gods in their own image.'[21] Similarly, 'The Negroes believe that their gods are flat nosed and black; the Thracians that their gods have blue eyes and red hair.'[22]

As Jaeger points out, Xenophanes represents the consciously critical side of the newly developed speculative philosophy. Although he comes from the Italian school of Greek philosophy, as the ancients called it, he is intellectually a child of the Ionians, and carries forward the critical implications of their philosophy for the traditional anthropomorphic and mythological religion. He goes beyond what we know of them in that he not only explicitly criticized the anthropomorphism of the old religion but attacked the moral implications of it as well. Homer, of whose influence and authority he was well aware—'he,' as he says, 'from whom all men have learnt in the beginning'—he, and Hesiod 'say that the gods do all manner of things which men would consider disgraceful—adultery, stealing, deceiving one another'.[23]

Against the older religion, Xenophanes puts forward a more religiously conscious version of the divinity of the Ionians. 'One god is the highest among gods and men; in neither his form or his thought is he like unto mortals.'[24] 'He sees as a whole, perceives as a whole, hears as a whole,'[25] and again, 'Always he remains in the same place, not moving at all, nor indeed does it benefit him to go here and there at different times; but without toil he makes all things shiver by the impulse of his mind.'[26] This is not explicit monotheism and there are difficulties regarding some of the other things Xenophanes says about his god—for instance, that he is spherical—but as later writers saw, it is not so very far removed.

That the new philosophical conception of god raised many difficulties, Xenophanes was in fact aware and he says at one point that with regard to thought about the highest questions there must always be an element of doubt;[27] but in the light of the positive theological statements in Xenophanes, it would be quite wrong to take this statement, as later Greek doxographers such as Sextus Empiricus did, as a statement of dogmatic agnosticism.

It is also worth noting that Xenophanes rejected divination. This is of a piece with his rejection of mythology and paves the way for the naturalistic explanation of this phenomenon which we come across in the medical writers of the latter part of the fifth century.

Sufficient has been said, I think, to show that Xenophanes can in no wise be regarded as either an atheist or an agnostic in our present day meanings of those terms. In fact, far from being either, he helps to lay the foundations for the subsequent development of the Greek conception of deity and thus exercised a considerable influence on later religious development.

Of the other great figures of the Pre-Socratic age, Pythagoras and Heraclitus fall well outside the limits of our inquiry
in that both were pre-eminently religious thinkers, and
Parmenides, while his influence upon naturalism was not inconsiderable, cannot really be regarded as a representative of
unbelief. He was not, as Armstrong notes, particularly
religious,[28] but the judgment of Karl Reinhardt that he is 'a
thinker who knows no other desire than knowledge, feels no
other manacle than logic, and is left indifferent by God and
by feeling'[29] fails to do justice to the positive theological side
of his reflections on the mystery of Being; and the religiously
charged imagery which we come across in the opening
section of Parmenides' poem, and which betrays obvious
Orphic influences, would seem also to tell against such an
extreme judgment.

Also in the Orphic tradition is the post-Parmenidean
thinker, Empedocles, though attempts have been made by
some, including the Roman Epicurean poet-philosopher
Lucretius, to represent him as a materialist, or at least to represent one side of his thought, usually taken as its mature expression, as materialistic, and as completely divorced from his
other, and primarily religious, side. The difficulty arises in that
we possess only fragments from two independent epic poems;
the one, *On Nature*, which is concerned to pursue the purely
physical side of the philosophy of nature, and the other, the
*Purifications* (or *Katharmoi*), which is a work of Orphic pietism.
It is on the basis of the former, of course, that Empedocles'
reputation as a materialist rests. The problem is thus that of
reconciling these two very disparate works as the products of
a unified mind. Some have attempted to assign the works to
two successive periods in Empedocles' life, the *Katharmoi*
being regarded by some as a work of adolescent fervour, later
abandoned, by others as the work of a last despairing period,
where, wearying of trying to explain the world in mechanical
terms, Empedocles is imagined as having thrown himself into

the arms of the irrational Orphic faith.[30] However, as both Jaeger and Guthrie, together with most recent commentators, show, when interpreted in the context of his times, these two aspects of his thought fit quite easily together.[31]

The other great post-Parmenidean thinker, Anaxagoras, a contemporary of Empedocles, is much more interesting. While in no sense an atheist, he did much to further the development of the naturalistic way of viewing events in the world. Whereas the diviners and priests of the traditional religion had interpreted events in nature, particularly the more freakish and spectacular, as caused by, and therefore as messages from, the gods, Anaxagoras firmly opposed this and sought for an explanation in terms of natural causes. The official reason for his banishment from Athens some few years before the birth of Plato was that he held that the heavenly bodies were natural objects. The sun, he said, was simply a glowing stone in the sky. But while Anaxagoras continued and strengthened that approach to the understanding of nature and natural processes which began with the Ionians over a century before, he took the remarkable step forward of identifying the first principle with Mind, although as Socrates pointed out, in that little piece of autobiography which we find recorded in the *Phaedo* where he tells us of the hope with which he turned to Anaxagoras' suggestion as a solution to his difficulties, he made singularly little use of it afterwards when he came to describe the workings of the world. But as Armstrong notes, Socrates' criticism is not, as it is often taken to be, that Anaxagoras limits the action of his Intelligence to that of starting motion in space, and then interpreting action in the world as being due to mechanical causes. It is that he made no attempt to explain the end or purpose of its activity, and how it ordered all things for the best.[32] Anaxagoras certainly held that the world was the product of an ordering Mind; what he failed to say was what the purposes of that Mind actually were. But in introducing the notion of an ordering Mind as the ground of the world, whether or not he himself actually identified it with divinity, he provides materials which Plato and his successors will not fail to develop in a theistic direction.

Diogenes of Apollonia, a contemporary of Anaxagoras, takes this argument a stage further. Accused by later writers not only of impiety but also of atheism, his position is in fact not unlike that of Anaxagoras, although he differs from him in returning to the approach of the Ionians and seeking for a single primary substance which in his case he takes to be air. This he further identifies with Mind. 'And it seems to me,' he says, 'that that which has the power of knowing is the thing that men call air, and that it steers all things and controls all things. For I feel that this is god, and that it extends everywhere and disposes all things and is contained in all things, and there is nothing that does not have a share in it.'[33] But not only does Diogenes explicitly refer to Mind as divine, he also goes beyond Anaxagoras in seeking to interpret individual phenomena in a purposeful or teleological manner, and it is highly probable that Socrates, in fact, takes from him that version of the teleological argument with which we find him, according to Xenophon's *Memorabilia*, seeking to refute the deism of one of his younger companions.

NOTES

[1] In *From Religion to Philosophy*, where Cornford traces the origin of Milesian philosophy and shows its emergence from the traditional religion.

[2] W. R. C. Guthrie, *History of Greek Philosophy* Vol 1, p 30

[3] *Ibid* p 26

[4] *Odyssey*, v 282

[5] Guthrie, *op cit* p 27

[6] Aristotle, *Metaphysics* A 983 b20

[7] Quoted with approval by Guthrie, *op cit* p 28

[8] *Ibid* p 29

[9] Burnet, *op cit* p 14

[10] W. Jaeger, *The Theology of the Early Greek Philosophers.* See pp v, 7–8 and 19–20.

[11] Guthrie, *op cit* pp 67–68. Though cf p 4 where he allows that the Ionians 'by no means excluded the possibility of divine agency' and adds, 'but they reached a conception of it very different from the conception of it in contemporary Greek society'.

[12] *Introduction to Ancient Philosophy* p 3

[13] Jaeger, *op cit* p 204

[14] *Ibid* p 36

[15] E. Gilson, *God and Philosophy* pp 4–5

[16] R. G. Collingwood, *The Idea of Nature* p 3. For a discussion of the Ionians, cf pp 29–48.

[17] A. N. Whitehead, *Adventures of Ideas* p 19

[18] F. Max-Müller, *Natural Religion* p 228

[19] *Op cit* p 13

[20] Frag 14

[21] Frag 15

[22] Frag 16

[23] Frag 11

[24] Frag 23

[25] Frag 24

[26] Frag 25 & 26

[27] Frag 34

[28] *Op cit* p 13

[29] Quoted Jaeger, *op cit* p 90

[30] Bide favours the first alternative and Diels the second.

[31] Jaeger, *op cit* p 130ff. Guthrie, *op cit* p 123ff of Vol II.

[32] *Op cit* p 17

[33] Frag B 5

# TWO

# THE SOCRATIC PERIOD

THE MENTION of Socrates brings us in fact to the latter part of the fifth century, to that period when the conflict between the implications of the newly developed natural philosophy and religion becomes open and explicit. The best evidence for this conflict and the issues which it raised comes from Plato who bent all his energies to combatting the irreligious implications of the new philosophy. But we can also get an insight into what must have been one of the great debates of the time from the dramatic writers of the period and especially from the comic playwright Aristophanes who takes this debate as the theme of his drama *The Clouds*.

But before looking at the philosophical issues let us look first, however, having mentioned the dramatists, at the evidence which we get from both Euripides and Sophocles of a growing moral criticism of the traditional religion and its stories of the gods. We have seen the beginnings of this line of criticism, about a century earlier, in Xenophanes. In Euripides and Sophocles it is very much to the fore. In passage after passage the doings of the gods, particularly as recorded in Homer, are the subject of moral disapproval. In fact as Lowes Dickinson says, the attitude of Euripides towards the popular religion 'is so frankly critical that . . . his main object in the construction of his dramas was to discredit the myths he selected for his theme'.[1] The reverse side of this can be seen in Sophocles and Aeschylus where it is evident that the moral development of Greek religion towards monotheism is not confined to the philosophers, but receives considerable impetus from the dramatic writers. A passage from Sophocles will illustrate this point. The Chorus is speaking:

*May destiny ever find me*
*pious in word and deed*
*prescribed by the laws that live on high:*
*laws begotten in the clear air of heaven,*
*whose only father is Olympus;*
*no mortal nature brought them to birth,*
*no forgetfulness shall lull them to sleep;*
*for God is great in them and grows not old.*[2]

Such words imply a complete transformation of the traditional conception of divinity.

To turn now to the philosophical issues, let us look first at the conflict between naturalism and mythology as it is presented by the comic dramatist Aristophanes. In the following passage, taken from *The Clouds*, the materialistic character of the physical understanding of nature current at the time is the main butt of his humour. Unfortunately, Socrates himself is cast in the role of advocate for the new naturalistic mode of explanation, but this misunderstanding of that philosopher's position need not deter us from seeing the point of the debate which follows. Others than Socrates certainly did take the position that Aristophanes is attacking. The passage referred to opens with a chorus from *The Clouds*, the new divinities of the physical philosophers, welcoming Socrates their protagonist. The dialogue which follows is between Strepsiades and Socrates:

STREPSIADES: Oh, earth! what a sound, how august and profound! it fills me with wonder and awe.
SOCRATES: (referring to the Clouds) These, these then alone, for true deities own, the rest are all god-ships of straw.
STREPS: Let Zeus be left out: He's a God beyond doubt; come, that you can scarcely deny.
SOCR: Zeus indeed! there's no Zeus: don't you be so obtuse.
STREPS: No Zeus up above in the sky?

Then you must first explain, who it is sends the rain;
or I really must think you are wrong.

SOCR: Well then, be it known, these send it alone: I can
prove it by argument strong.

Was there ever a shower seen to fall in an hour when
the sky was all cloudless and blue?

Yet on a fine day, when the clouds are away, he might
send one according to you.

STREPS: Well, it must be confessed, that chimes in with the
rest: your words I am forced to believe.

Yet before I had dreamed that the rain water streamed
from Zeus and his chamber-pot sieve.

But whence then, my friend, does the thunder descend?
that it makes us quake with affright!

SOCR: Why, 'tis they I declare, as they roll through the air.

STREPS: What the clouds? did I hear you aright?

SOCR: Ay: for when to the brim filled with water they
swim, by Necessity carried along,

They are hung up on high in the vault of the sky, and so
by Necessity strong

In the midst of their course, they clash with great force,
and thunder away without end.

STREPS: But is it not He who compels this to be? does not
Zeus this Necessity send?

SOCR: No Zeus have we there, but a vortex of air.

STREPS: What! Vortex? that's something I own.

I knew not before, that Zeus was no more, but Vortex
was placed on his throne . . .[3]

And so the debate continues through a naturalistic explanation of the causes of other events in nature and the suggestion
is further made that the atheist who offers such an explanation
is anti-social and immoral. But our interest is in the issue of
natural as against mythological explanations of natural
phenomena and the above passage, comedy aside, brings out

well the type of explanation in terms of physical causes operating according to necessity which the new philosophy of
nature was putting forward in opposition to the explanations
of the traditional religious mythology.

It was just such causal explanations with which Socrates
professed himself dissatisfied in that piece of his autobiography
which we find in Plato's dialogue *The Phaedo*. 'When I was
a young man,' says Socrates to Cebe, 'I was wonderfully
desirous of that wisdom which they call a history of nature:
for it appeared to me to be a very sublime thing to know the
causes of everything, why each thing is generated, why it
perishes and why it exists.'[4] The works of Anaxagoras particularly seemed to offer what he was looking for, for here
was a philosopher who 'said that it is intelligence that sets in
order and is the cause of all things'. 'I was delighted,' Socrates
goes on, 'with this cause and it appeared to me in a manner to
be well that intelligence should be the cause of all things.'

His delight was short lived, and he tells the story of his dis-
illusionment. 'From this wonderful hope . . . I was speedily
thrown down, when, as I advanced and read over his works,
I met with a man who makes no use of intelligence, nor
assigns any causes for the ordering of all things, but makes
the cause to consist of air, ether and water and many other
things equally absurd.' Socrates illustrates what he means by
reference to his own actions. Anaxagoras appears to him to
be the sort of person who would explain Socrates' remaining
in Athens, facing imprisonment and death, not by saying that
he wished and had good reasons for doing so, but by reference
to his physiological constitution. To call such an explanation
is, he says, absurd, though as he recognizes, 'if anyone should
say that without possessing such things as bones and sinews,
and whatever else I have, I could not do what I pleased, he
would speak the truth'.

The point I take it of what Socrates is saying is that a causal
explanation along the lines offered by the physical philosophers

is a limited explanation and does nothing to satisfy those who are asking other and different questions; who are asking for an explanation in terms of meaning and purpose; who are asking, as Socrates himself expresses it, for reasons rather than causes, and for what Aristotle was later to call the final cause of the workings of things.

This is the point at issue and it is a point which will recur when in the seventeenth century the search for final causes, for a transcendent intelligible meaning in the universe, which had been revived in the Middle Ages, begins to recede and an explanation of events, not dissimilar to that sought by the old physical philosophers, reappears.

Further evidence of the widespread nature of the empirical and naturalistic way of explaining events in the middle of the fifth century is provided by the medical writers of the period whose works have come down to us under the name of Hippocrates. Of the importance of these writings for the understanding of naturalism F. M. Cornford and others have made us aware.[5] In one of the most well-known treatises of this school 'On the Nature of the Sacred Disease', as epilepsy was called, the empirically minded author inquires into the so-called divine origin of this disease and raises thereby some important questions about the nature of the divine and the mode of its operation. He disposes of the mythological idea that epilepsy is the direct result of divine activity and seeks to account for it as being the result of the same kind of natural causes as are other diseases. 'The so-called sacred disease,' he writes, 'arises from the same causes as any others: from the things that enter the body and those that leave it: from cold, and sunshine, and winds, which are always changing and are never still. These things are divine; and so there is no need of setting this disease apart and considering it more divine than the others: they are all divine and they are all human.'[6]

It is interesting to compare this with that sober minded

empirical approach to the writing of history which we find at this time in Thucydides. If we compare his account of the Peloponnesian war with accounts of similar happenings in Homer or Herodotus we cannot fail to notice the difference between them. Whereas in Homer and Herodotus we find natural and supernatural causation operating side by side, we find nothing of this in Thucydides who eliminates the supernatural element altogether and gives us an account of the war in ordinary terms. As Drachmann says, 'Not only did he throughout ignore omens and divinations, except in so far as they played a part as a purely psychological factor, but he completely omitted a reference to the gods in his narrative. Such a procedure was at this time unprecedented.'[7]

This is an approach to the writing and understanding of history which has only really succeeded in establishing itself in our own day.

But the middle of the fifth century is supremely the age of the Sophists and while with them interest shifts away from the object of knowledge to the subject, from the external world to the life of man in society, the scepticism of the age is in them even more pronounced. Religion, morality and society are all subjected to devastating criticism. Whether or no the opprobrium which Plato has cast on the name is justified by the actual teachings of such men as Gorgias, Protagoras and Prodicus may well be doubted, but that they subjected, for good or ill, the foundations of the traditional structure of society in religion and morality to searching criticism and put little that was positive in its place is an established fact. On the whole their teaching, which consisted for the most part of rhetoric, was designed to enable the young to succeed in public life. Armstrong describes their beliefs as those of 'a humanistic agnosticism',[8] and this would appear to be justified both by their expressed remarks as they have come down to us and by the relativistic position which they took both with regard to religion and morality. Protagoras expresses their outlook when he makes man 'the measure of all things, of the reality of those which are, and of the unreality of those which are not'—a saying which the apostles of humanism have taken to themselves ever since. With regard to the question of the existence of the gods, Protagoras is frankly agnostic and his judgment here is one which many since his time have echoed with heartfelt intensity. 'With regard to the gods I cannot feel sure either that they are, or that they are not, nor what they are like in figure, for there are many things that hinder sure knowledge: the obscurity of the subject and the shortness of human life.'[9] Drachmann thinks that Protagoras was the first to pose this question as an open one which might admit of a negative answer.

The Sophists took up and answered a question which had been the subject of debate before their time but which they themselves raised with a new intensity. Contact with other cultures had made the Greeks aware for some time that their own culture, with its religion and its morality and its political and social organization, was not unique even though it might to them be superior. Reflecting on the diversity of beliefs in the world with regard to these things they were led to ask whether religion, morality and social structure were inherent in the nature of things so that there was one true form of them or whether they were simply the outcome of custom and therefore relative and subject to change. As they themselves put it; were these things of nature or of law? The Sophists had no hesitation in choosing the latter alternative. Religion and morality and society were for them simply a matter of man-made customs. This had the interesting corollary that it allowed them not only to attack religion, but to go one step further and offer a naturalistic account of its origin. A number of such theories have come down to us. One of the most important of the Sophists, Prodicus of Cos, puts forward the view, to which both Euripides and the Stoical writer Lucilus Balbus later refer, that the ideas of the gods arose as an act of gratitude and adoration on man's part towards the beneficent powers of nature. Thus the earliest gods for Prodicus were such ones as Ceres, Liber, Demeter and Dionysus.

Somewhat later, one of their younger followers, the cynical and nihilistic Critias, in his now lost drama *Sisyphus*, holds what we might term the 'policeman' theory of the gods. They were invented, he says, as moral authorities to end lawlessness. To fully appreciate this we need to be aware of the part which 'witnesses' played in the morality of the period. Laws, the Sophists held, were the creation of the arbitrary will of rulers and they contrasted this with natural justice in which the will of the stronger prevailed. It was thus held by them that men would act differently in the absence of any possibility of detection, that is, of witnesses. Plato raises this question in his story of Gyges' ring[10] which would make its wearer invisible. Critias' view was that the gods were invented as hidden witnesses to acts done in private in order to provide the necessary coercion without which morality as we know it would disintegrate.

Another thinker who offers us a naturalistic theory of the origin of religion, although this time combined with a materialistic theory of nature is the Atomist Democritus, a man who is in no wise a Sophist in the traditional meaning of that term. Democritus retains much of the old Ionian and post-Parmenidean interest in nature and natural processes. Where he goes beyond these is in his rejection of any form of divinity either outside of or within nature. As Jaeger says, 'His description of nature in terms of the interplay of countless atoms in empty space ruled by the power of chance left no room for teleology and the deification of any moving forces or single primal ground.'[11] In Democritus, as many have pointed out, the naturalistic implications of Ionian philosophy of nature reach their final and logical conclusion and we have an explicit statement of what, as F. M. Cornford puts it, 'the philosophers call materialism and religious people call atheism'.[12]

Yet the existence in men's minds of conceptions of the divine and of the gods created for Democritus, as it was later to create for Epicurus, who worked with his natural philosophy, an epistemological problem. How could the ideas of the gods be accounted for? Democritus offers us in fact two theories. The first relegates the gods to 'a twilight realm of materialized psychical phenomena',[13] for what Democritus suggests is that the images of the gods, which he calls 'eidola' arise from dreams, more particularly from dreams arising out of a bad conscience where the gods appear as the punishers of the evil deeds of men. Democritus thus recognized not only their effectiveness in the life of man, but also the place of prayer, which he said could be regarded as a wish to encounter propitious images, and it is thus linked with morality, although Democritus' own faith in morality in the absence of religion rests in his faith in the moral force of a man's inner sense of self-respect.[14]

His other theory of the origin of religion is that it arises from man's awe and fear of the wonders of nature. Like many today he no doubt believed that once the natural origin of these was fully understood religious belief would be seen to be unfounded.

It should also be added that Democritus did not believe in any life after death, holding that everything in nature is subject to decay and dissolution.

The moral use to which Democritus' views were put by Epicurus we shall look at shortly.

I shall conclude this section of our inquiry with the story which is told about that typical atheist of later antiquity, Diagoras of Melos. It is said that he became an atheist, not from speculation but from the experience of having lost a manuscript and of having prayed unsuccessfully to the gods for its return. Unfortunately little else is known of him except that he was condemned to death in 415 BC in Athens, having been arrested for scoffing at the Eleusinian Mysteries.

We thus come to the end of our survey of unbelief in the Pre-Socratic and Socratic period; the period which covers the two centuries from the beginning of the sixth to the end of the fifth century BC. Two things I think ought to be borne in mind. We see on the one hand from the Ionians onwards the development of a naturalism which reaches its zenith in the Atomism of Democritus and which in the latter part of the fifth century is reinforced by the relativistic criticism of the Sophists. On the other hand we can discern the beginnings of a more sophisticated conception of the divine which will in Plato and Aristotle to a large extent displace the traditional religion and in its later developments become a genuine alternative to it.

But alongside these, the intellectual currents of the age, the traditional religion continues to survive and flourish in its manifold variety together with Orphism and the Mysteries and innumerable other cults and practices. The influence of the philosophical debate on popular piety is of course impossible to determine.

Plato and Aristotle fall well outside the scope of our inquiry. Plato's philosophy is inspired by a moral and metaphysical vision which is thoroughly religious both in intention and execution as well as being motivated by a desire to combat the secular minded freethinking of the day. Aristotle is rather more difficult to assess, in that his theology bears so little relationship to the rest of his philosophy—the more so where his ethics are concerned. In many ways he is the precursor of the deism which comes to dominate certain subsequent periods of theology. His vision is very much this-worldly and while his God, whom he describes as the 'Unmoved Mover', draws the world to Himself by his inherent perfection, He is for the most part simply a metaphysical postulate, very much the 'God of the philosophers' against which so many advocates of religion have, with Pascal, complained. The influence of his naturalistic, not to say rationalistic approach, both to nature and to politics and ethics will be felt throughout Europe when his works reappear during the mediaeval period, and we shall consider their implications and the questions which they raise in chapter six.

NOTES

[1] *Op cit* p 48
[2] Sophocles, *Oedipus The King* 865.
[3] Aristophanes, *The Clouds* 358.
[4] *Phaedo*, 96ff. Quotations are taken from the Everyman Library Edition p 185ff of Plato *Five dialogues*. Edit. by A. D. Lindsay.
[5] Cf his essay on the Hippocratic school in his book, *Principium Sapientiae*.
[6] Hippocrates, *On the Sacred Disease*, Chapt 21
[7] *Op cit* p 28
[8] *Op cit* p 23
[9] Frag 4
[10] *Republic*, Bk II 359–60
[11] *Op cit* p 180
[12] Cornford, *Before and After Socrates* p 27
[13] Jaeger, *op cit* p 181
[14] Cf Stob iv. 5, 46 (Democritus 264)

# THREE

# THE HELLENISTIC AGE

THE HELLENISTIC AGE, the age when the culture and civilization of Greece, following in the wake of Alexander of Macedon's conquests, breaks out of the confines of its native environment and comes to dominate the thinking of the Mediterranean world, sees the rise of four great schools of philosophical thought which more or less successfully challenge the Platonic and Aristotelian schools. These are the Stoic, the Cynic, the Epicurean and the Sceptical schools. Of these the Stoic was for the most part pantheistic—a peculiar blend of Platonic thought about providence, a good deal of Aristotle, and a language reminiscent of the Ionian doctrine of 'living-stuff'. All men, it taught, participate in God or the Divine by means of their reason, the divine spark—the *logos spermatikos*—which is within them. The whole universe is in fact divine, originating from the primal divine fire and ultimately destined to return to it. On the whole the Stoic influence was in the field of morality, where as time went by and its morality freed itself from its theological grounding, it eventually came to dominate the field and influence some of the best minds of late antiquity.

The Cynic philosophy, founded by Diogenes of Sinope, a contemporary of Aristotle, was primarily a way of life based upon the doctrine that virtue, interpreted as life according to nature, is the one thing that matters and that all else is *tuphos* or wind. Of Diogenes it is recorded that he did not take part in the worship of the gods because the gods were in need of nothing, but any further theological opinions that he might have expressed have not come down to us. On the whole the Cynic attitude is best described as one of indifference on religious matters and as such it can be described as practically atheistic though theoretically agnostic.

The philosophies of Epicureanism and Scepticism are much more interesting from our point of view; the former in that many people have looked back to it as one of the great humanistic and secular philosophies of Antiquity,[1] the latter because in many respects, when taken in conjunction with the scepticism of the Middle Platonic Academy, it is the precursor of a scepticism which we shall see revived at the Renaissance and again in the eighteenth century by David Hume and the philosophical tradition which he initiated and which survives as one of the dominating philosophical approaches of today.

Lucretius, writing in the first century before Christ, looks back to Epicurus, the founder of the philosophy which bears his name, and who had died over a century earlier in 270 BC, and hails him as the great liberator of the human spirit from the yoke of the superstitions of religion in these words. 'When human life lay grovelling in all men's sight, crushed to the earth under the dead weight of superstition whose grim features loured menacingly upon mortals from the four quarters of the sky, a man of Greece was the first to raise mortal eyes in defiance, first to stand erect and brave the challenge. Fables of the gods did not crush him, nor the lightning flash and the growing menace of the sky. Rather they quickened his manhood, so that he, first of all men, longed to smash the constraining locks of nature's doors. The vital vigour of his mind prevailed. He ventured far out beyond the flaming ramparts of the world and voyaged in mind throughout infinity. Returning victorious, he proclaimed to us what can be and what cannot: how a limit is fixed to the power of everything and an immovable frontier post. Therefore, superstition in its turn lies crushed beneath his feet, and we by his triumph are lifted level with the skies.'[2]

Epicurus' philosophical interests are, like those of the Stoics, primarily moral and he, like them, sought for a way of living which would, amidst the troubled times in which he lived produce *ataraxia* or *apatheia*, imperturbability and peace. With this moral search he combined the old Ionian interest in nature and made the latter, as it developed into Atomism, the basis of the former. Believing as he did that what most militated against the inner calmness of mind and emotion for which he strove were the superstitions of religion—fear of the gods and of what might await one after death—he found in the Atomism of Democritus a philosophy which, with its materialistic outlook, excluded just those sources of so much pain and trouble. Thus, embracing the materialism of Democritus, the wise man could draw from his naturalistic picture of the world peace and self-reliance.

But while his philosophy is atheistic to all intents and purposes, Epicurus himself, curiously enough admitted the existence of the gods of the traditional religion. They were, of course, material like everything else, but they were also everlasting. His theology is quite original and arises, in fact, quite naturally from the basic materialistic premises of his system. With Democritus, Epicurus sought to account for the fact that men not only believed in the gods but also claimed to have been the recipients of 'visions' of them. His theory was that the gods, though invisible to the normal eye, were made of finer stuff than were the objects of our normal experience of the world—a stuff more akin to that out of which souls were compounded. Thus the atoms which the gods gave off penetrated into our minds and gave rise to the 'images' of the gods which were experienced in sleep and trance. Epicurus' gods, however, take no part in the affairs of the world and can at the most act as an ideal for human life—the life of an Epicurean philosopher.

The last and in many ways the most important school of the post-Aristotelian period to lay claim to our attention is that of the Sceptics. The origins of this school go back to Pyrrho of Elis, a contemporary of Aristotle, and it is from him that the term 'Pyrrhonism' is derived—a term which from this time onwards until about the close of the nineteenth century was the common designation for such scepticism. Pyrrho himself has left us no exposition of his views. It is from his disciple, Timon of Phlius, that his views have come down to us. His position, in so far as we can reconstruct it, would appear to be that as nothing can be known with complete certainty we should neither affirm nor deny anything. This led naturally to his taking an agnostic position with regard to religious belief. Pyrrho's scepticism, however, was motivated primarily by the search for tranquillity which he believed would follow from realizing perfect suspension of judgment—a form of scepticism which was to be revived by Aenesidemus in the first century BC and which in the second century AD was to produce that fine flowering of ancient scepticism that we find in Sextus Empiricus.

Another source of Scepticism is found in the later developments within the Platonic Academy, though unlike the scepticism of Pyrrho it is characterized by a more thoroughly destructive dialectical spirit and while initially this destructive dialectic was used against the arguments of the Stoics—known to the Sceptics as 'The Dogmatists'—as a weapon it was capable of being adapted for use against all forms of dogmatism, philosophical and religious.

It was Arcesilaus who, towards the opening of the second century BC, introduced Sceptical doctrines into the Platonic Academy, and so founded the second or Middle Academy, as it is known. He, it would appear, was led from his criticism of Stoic criteria of truth to maintain that there could not be any criteria of truth and so no certainty with regard to anything. The most that could be hoped for was probability, what he termed 'ta euloga', the reasonable. Whether this led to complete scepticism with regard to religion is not known.

But about the sceptical attitude to religion of his successor,

Carneades of Cyrene (213-129 BC), we are in no doubt, as both Cicero and Sextus Empiricus, two later Sceptics, have made us well acquainted with his views.[3] With regard to religious belief, as with regard to anything else, there could, he held, be no certainty. But Carneades' criticism of religion, and of theism in particular, went far deeper than this and in one respect at least he anticipates a discussion with reference to the concept of God which is still very much alive in contemporary criticism of theism today.

Stoic theology was not unlike Christian theology, which indeed it influenced, in many vital respects. Integral to them both is a teleological theory of the universe based upon a belief in God and His providential care for man and the ordering of events in the world to this end. It was this, in its Stoic version, that Carneades set himself to criticize.

Inquiring into the evidence offered in support of such views Carneades began by attempting to refute the evidence drawn from theism's universality—the first argument in the Stoic's apologia, and the argument mentioned in the Introduction to this book. If belief in the gods is universal, Carneades argued, why bother to rest it on argument and risk suggesting that it might indeed be a matter for debate? While himself doubting the fact of the universality of the belief, what, should its universality be granted, Carneades asked, is proved? And his answer is that all that would be proved is the sociological or anthropological fact that men believe in the existence of the gods; further argument is needed to show that the gods do in fact exist. A simple, but important, logical point. He argues further that questions of truth are not to be decided by plebiscite, by counting heads. It is somewhat odd he says, for the Stoics, who for the most part regarded the mass of mankind as little more than fools, to commit such an important question to its judgment.

The evidence for theism—or to be more accurate here, for polytheism—drawn from the appearances of the gods to men, and from divination, Carneades also dismisses; the former summarily, as little more than old wives' tales; the latter, in view of the respect in which it was held, with more argument. He concentrates upon the arbitrariness of divination. If it were a way of foretelling events it would rest on rational principles and not upon routine and tradition. As it stands it is little more than a hit or miss affair owing nothing to divine inspiration.

Carneades himself believes that belief in the existence of the gods arose, for the most part, from the deification of awe inspiring natural phenomena—though once again he shows us the logical subtlety of his mind by pointing out that the question of the origin of a belief tells us nothing of itself about the validity of that belief. This is a point not without contemporary interest at a time when so many regard the question of the existence of God as settled negatively once an account of the origin of the belief in this proposition has been put forward—usually today in psychological or sociological terms. The point that Carneades is making is that we must distinguish between 'reasons' and 'causes' with regard to the beliefs that people hold. The causes only become interesting and important, as a means of accounting for a person holding the belief that he does, when we have come to the conclusion that, irrespective of the causes, there are no reasons that might justify the holding of that belief.

With regard to belief in the existence of the gods, Carneades argues that this is in fact the case. Indeed he goes further, and in a vein reminiscent of some of the recent criticisms of theism, he argues that the concept of God, at least as put forward by the Stoics, is not only false but meaningless, in that it is self-contradictory—or, as modern philosophers would say, internally inconsistent. His arguments, however, are not confinable simply to the Stoic conception of the deity. As Mr R. D. Hicks has pointed out in his study of Carneades' philosophy of religion, 'this acute thinker used arguments which go much further than this and bring to light the fundamental difficulties in any conception of God, whether He be conceived as personal or impersonal, finite or infinite or veiled under some abstraction as the absolute or the unconditioned'.[4] Quite simply what Carneades argued is that we cannot ascribe to God personal attributes without limiting his nature. Yet God as traditionally conceived by the Stoics (and of course by Jews and Christians) is both unlimited and infinite, and yet personal. To go fully into Carneades' reasoning here would take us too far afield, but I shall give one example to illustrate the kind of approach which Carneades brought to bear upon this problem. God, it was said by the Stoics, is a rational being endowed with all excellence. But virtue, as we understand it, is incompatible with this, for virtue presupposes imperfection overcome. For example, to be courageous one must have been exposed to danger; to be temperate, pleasure must have been resisted. How, asks Carneades, can God exhibit such virtue? How can a Being who is omnipotent face danger and who is passionless resist pleasure which does not affect Him? Does He then lack the virtues of fortitude and temperance? If He does then how can He be described as all-virtuous. We can't have our cake and eat it, or put more philosophically, affirm and deny, of the same subject, some attribute or other. Carneades has much more to say about the other attributes of God, his infinity and his rationality, for instance, that is in the same vein.

Before leaving our discussion of him we must say something about his attack on the Stoic conception of divine providence, for in attacking this doctrine he is also attacking—in a vein similar to that which David Hume will employ in the eighteenth century—the Argument from Design. The evidence for design in the world Carneades regards as inconclusive and he points to those features of the world which would seem to tell against its being the outcome of design on the part of a divine Designer—poisonous snakes, destructive agencies on land and sea, disease and so on. God's greatest gift to man is held to be his reason. But why, if God is providential, has this gift been so unevenly and unfairly distributed? Is God guilty of partiality in his dealings with men? No. For Carneades, as for Hume and later for John Stuart Mill, the most reasonable conclusion would appear to be to deny the existence of God—or—what amounts virtually to the same thing—to maintain that if there is a God we can neither know nor say anything about him. Hicks' comment on Carneades would therefore seem justified when he says that 'it is curious to observe how far Carneades has anticipated much of subsequent metaphysic, his reasoned objections when translated into English run almost insensibly into modern philosophical language'.[5]

There is one other figure whom we must consider before we pass from the Hellenistic period to that of the early Roman empire and that is Euhemerus, the thinker who has given his name to that theory of the origin of the gods, known as Euhemerism, which holds that the gods are simply glorified heroes from times long passed. Little, however, is known of him, but his theory that the gods were simply the older heroes of the Greek folk tradition is not one that is entirely original, for that tradition had always believed that the gods came into existence in time and lived, in their own region of the world, a life not entirely out of character with that of the heroes of old. Hecataeus somewhat earlier had also maintained that all excellent men became gods. Euhemerus' doctrine, however, fell on fertile soil, and it was one destined to persist for a long time to come. In the Roman world of the second century AD Diodorus seized, in his history, upon Euhemerism as the best scientific explanation of religion and many others, notable among them Thomas Carlyle as late as the last century, have followed this line of thought.

## NOTES

1 Cf for instance H. J. Blackham in his recently published, *Humanism* p 107ff

2 Lucretius, *De Rerum Natura*. Trans by R. E. Latham, Penguin Classics edit, p 29.

3 Cf Cicero, *On the Nature of the Gods*, III. Sextus Empiricus, *Against the Mathematicians*, IX.

4 R. D. Hicks, *Stoic and Epicurean* p 330

5 *Op cit* p 337

# FOUR

# THE ROMAN PERIOD

DURING THE PERIOD of the early Roman Empire which covers the last century BC and the first two centuries of the Christian era, while the great philosophical schools of the post-Aristotelian period persist, and the most notable of them, the Platonic, undergoes a great revival, there are also a number of figures who come before us as the exponents of an approach to life which strikes us as on the whole secular or humanistic. They are not unfortunately great or original thinkers. Their approach is that of civilized and urbane men and what philosophy there is underlying their approach to life is for the most part drawn from Greek sources. The three leading figures are Cicero, Lucretius and Pliny the Elder. But first a word about the time in which they lived. The Roman state recognized the importance of religion as a bulwark for morality—particularly so far as the masses of their subjects were concerned. At a later stage it also became a test of political orthodoxy. Yet, as Glover notes in his book *The Conflict of Religions in the Early Roman Empire*, there has hardly existed an age less interested in religion—unless of course it be our own. Glover is, of course, referring to the educated upper classes. Their secularism and cynicism is typified in Cicero. For instance, writing to his wife from exile, he says, 'If however these misfortunes are permanent, then, my darling, I wish to see you as soon as possible and to die in your embrace, since neither the gods whom you have worshipped . . . nor men whom I have always served, have requited us.'[1] As others have noted, Cicero had no other religion than philosophy, his consolation in adversity and his guide to the conduct of life. Philosophically, he stood with the sceptically minded Academics, though his

philosophy of religion can fairly be called Stoic. As a statesman, he stood by the established Roman religion, as his works
on *The State* and *The Laws* show, but such adherence was
purely political, and we can say that to all intents and purposes
he is a practical, if not a theoretical, atheist. Drachmann, too,
notes that such an attitude was widespread among the upper
classes at the beginning of the Christian era, an age in which
philosophy and particularly ethical philosophy was prominent,
and in which religion was not so much opposed as ignored as
irrelevant to the real problems of life.[2] The poet Horace is
every whit as secular minded, laughing in his *Odes* at both
superstition and at any suggestion of a divine interest in
men.

Yet while an informed interest in religion was remote from
the thinking of the upper classes, this was a period not only of
religious fervour on the part of the masses who flocked to the
newly imported Phrygian, Egyptian and other Oriental cults,
but towards the close, one in which the need for religion on
the part of this section of the community was satisfied to a
great extent by the newly established Christian sect.

Among the thinkers who did in fact rise to a philosophical
articulation of unbelief we must not overlook Lucretius, and
at a later date Pliny the Elder.

Lucretius we have already mentioned as looking back to
Epicurus for his inspiration. His attitude as we have it in his
superb poem *On The Nature of the Universe*—he is the only
European writer who has ever put a philosophical system, as
distinct from a theological one, into great poetry—is one of
complete atheism. His attitude is that of one who is reconciled
to life by the calm contemplation of law as it reigns in the
universe and by the knowledge that the gods do not exist and
that all life ends in death. Religion, he holds, is guilty of many
misdeeds, not least of human sacrifice, and so ought to be
abolished entirely. Yet, on the other hand, he is aware of the
poetic power of nature and not at times unsympathetic to,

although he cannot support, arguments from the other side which speak of a divine power in nature.

In Pliny the Elder we again find a pantheism which identifies God and the Universe to such an extent that Drachmann in his study of *Atheism in Pagan Antiquity*, to which we have referred, is led to describe him as an atheist, and certainly it would appear, in the passage from his *History*, which Drachmann quotes, that his attitude to the divine is one of indifference to say the least. He writes, 'I therefore deem it a sign of human weakness to ask about the shape or form of God. Whoever God is, if any other God (than the universe) exists at all, and in whatever part of the world he is, he is all perception, all sight, all hearing, all soul, all reason, all self.'[3] This is Stoic pantheism carried to its logical conclusion, and Drachmann holds that this was the point that the educated Roman classes of the early Empire had reached under Hellenistic influence. Glover, too, describes the Stoicism of the period, by which almost all the upper classes were influenced, as, for all practical purposes, atheistic. Everything was thrown on the individual will. He writes, 'If the gods, as Seneca claims, lend a hand to such a climb, the climber has to make his own way by temperance and fortitude. The "holy spirit within us" is after all hardly to be distinguished from conscience, intellect and will. God, says Epictetus, ordains that if you wish for good, get it for yourself.'[4] So also Seneca, 'What do you want with prayers?' he asks, 'make yourself happy.'[5]

The Stoics of this period have little that is definite to say about either polytheism or the personality of the gods. 'God', 'the gods', 'Zeus' are used interchangeably and more often than not identified with fate, nature and the universe. Thus, Stoicism fell, as Glover points out, between two stools. On the one hand it hadn't a sufficient feeling for the past to give any support to popular religion, nor, on the other, the resolution to be done with it. It vacillated.

The greatest representative, after Epictetus, of the Stoicism of this period, is of course the Emperor, Marcus Aurelius. The agnosticism and practical atheism which we have noted as characterizing the Stoicism of others is present to an even higher degree in him, so much so that, as F. W. Myers has said, 'The peculiar mind of the solitary Emperor has made him the saint and the exemplar of Agnosticism.' He is, says Glover, a man 'who neither believes nor disbelieves—"either gods or atoms" seems to be the necessary antithesis, and there is so much to be said both for or against each of the alternatives that decision is impossible'.[6]

The poets of the first two centuries of the Christian Era also join in the general attitude of agnosticism and cynicism towards religion. Oenomas in his *The Swindlers Unmasked* violently attacks the oracles as a priestly fraud. More significant, however, is Lucian in whom many have seen a prefiguration of Voltaire, although he differs from Voltaire in having less purpose and no definite principles. Religious belief for Lucian was nothing if not ridiculous and therefore a fitting subject for his light satires, in which he ridiculed belief in the gods. His *Lover of Lies* takes the gods at their face value and reduces the situations described in the traditional religion to absurdity. Zeus, at one point, 'most amiably allows him to stand and watch him at work, hearing prayers as they come up through tubes, and granting or rejecting them, then settling some auguries, and finally arranging the weather'.[7] His *Zeus Tragoedus* and *Zeus Elenchomenus* are written in the same vein. In the former the gods are pictured as listening to a debate on earth concerning their existence which they finally settle with a good shower of thunderbolts. Lucian, however, is not a serious thinker. His questions, as Glover remarks, are lightly asked and lightly answered, and if we look to him for anything other than a satire on the popular religion we look in vain.[8]

One thinker remains before we come to the end of our survey of unbelief in Classical Antiquity and that is the late second and early third century figure of Sextus Empiricus. Sextus is not only the last and the greatest of the thinkers in the Sceptical tradition, he is also one of our chief sources for what knowledge we have of the early period of philosophy. Sextus is a sceptic in the Epicurean tradition seeking that freedom from mental excitement which will secure him peace of mind. Morally he seeks for a position beyond the struggle of good and evil. 'The sceptic,' he writes, 'does away with the opinion that anything is evil in its nature.' Two works have come down to us from him and their titles are significant, *The Pyrrhonic Institutes* and *Against the Dogmatists*. Of them, Robert Flint, in his monumental *Study of Agnosticism* has this to say. 'All Greek Scepticism, all that was important in the most thorough and consistent development of agnosticism which has appeared in the world, seems to have been preserved in them.'[9] Their influence on later thinkers has been considerable. The Scepticism which we shall see revived in Europe from about the beginning of the sixteenth century draws its inspiration, its principles, its methods and indeed its arguments largely from his writings. Montaigne and Hume in particular quoted extensively from him. So also did Sir Walter Raleigh.[10]

The conclusions, however, which the Sceptics of the classical period drew with regard to religious practice tended towards support for the 'status quo'. Thus even Sextus, while arguing philosophically against the reasonableness of religious belief (and of course, unbelief, being, as he was, a consistent agnostic!) professed at the same time his faith in the gods and in their providential concern for mankind. He writes, 'The Sceptic will be found acknowledging the gods according to the customs of his country and the laws and doing everything that tends to their proper worship and reverence, but in the region of philosophic enquiry he makes no rash assertion.'[11] So Cotta, who holds the position of pontifex in the Roman constitution and whom Cicero casts in the role of Sceptic in his *de Natura Deorum*, can say, 'I have always defended and will always defend the traditional ceremonies of religion . . . if you, as a philosopher can justify my belief on rational grounds, good but I am bound to believe our ancestors, even though they give no reason.'[12]—after saying which he proceeds to demolish the proofs which the Stoic has adduced for Divine providence by means of arguments drawn from Carneades.

This position of private unbelief and public profession of faith is one which many in positions of responsibility in subsequent ages were to make their own.

## NOTES

[1] Cicero, *Ad Fam* 14.4. Quoted p 223 of *Latin Literature in Translation* by Kevin Guinagh and Alfred P. Dorjahn.

[2] *Op cit* p 116

[3] Quoted Drachmann *op cit* p 118 cf Pliny *Natural History*, II. 1–27 ss 14.

[4] *Op cit* p 65

[5] *Ibid* p 66

[6] *Ibid* p 198

[7] Glover, *ibid* p 209 cf Lucian. 1 *Caromen* 24.

[8] But cf Edwyn Bevan, *Stoics and Sceptics* p 138 for a much higher estimate of Lucian's worth.

[9] Rober Flint, *Agnosticism* p 95

[10] Cf G. T. Buckley, *Atheism in the English Renaissance* Chapt XI

[11] *Ad Math.* IX. 49

[12] *Op cit* Bk 14

# FIVE

# CONCLUSION

BEFORE CLOSING this first section of our enquiry it will be as well to cast our minds back over the period we have been reviewing and to take note of the major trends towards unbelief. Five major points emerge. But first a general remark. Our avowed purpose is the study of atheism and agnosticism and is might appear that in the preceding pages we have wandered from this in that we have been able to instance very few examples of avowed and explicit atheism and not many more, except towards the close of the period, of agnosticism. However, it is during this period, as I have tried to show, that we find the beginnings of both the naturalistic and the sceptical outlook on life which will play so large a part subsequently in the development of a fuller and explicit atheism. Which brings me to my first point.

The naturalistic understanding of events in the world which was begun by the Ionian philosophers, and instances of which we have found also in the medical writings of the fifth century, as well as in Thucydides' approach to the writing of history, and which was brought to fruition by the Atomists and was a major topic of debate during the Socratic period, is a form of understanding which we shall find re-occurring at subsequent periods in Western thought. It is also not without contemporary interest in so far as the issues which it raises for theism are still very much alive today. Much contemporary theological language is still 'mythological'—unashamedly so—in that events in the world are interpreted in terms of a mixed, natural and supernatural, language. Rudolf Bultmann, the great German theologian, who has done so much to 'de-mythologize' religious language, contrasts the religious under-

standing with that of modern science in which the cause-
effect nexus is fundamental. 'Modern men take it for granted,'
he says, 'that the course of nature and of history, like their own
inner life and their practical life, is nowhere interrupted by the
intervention of supernatural powers.'[1] The legitimacy or
otherwise of what is known as 'interventionist language',
which Bultmann, John Robinson and others have done so much
to discredit today, it is not our intention to discuss, but it is
interesting to discover that the points raised against such language by theologians in our own day were first raised over
two thousand years ago. They are fundamental to the philosophy of religion. Are events in the world to be understood
as resulting from natural causes only or can we discern in
events, either taken individually or together, divine activity
and purpose? Traditional Judæo-Christian Faith has answered
this question affirmatively. There is, it says, divine purpose
and providence in the world and some events are the result
of direct divine intervention. But the whole course of development in our understanding of the world, at least from
the sixteenth century, has been rightly or wrongly away from
this way of looking at the world. The origins of this alternative
approach lie, as I hope I have shown, in the Classical period.
It is this period's most significant contribution to the development of atheism.

The second point to notice during the Classical period is the
growing moral criticism of traditional religion, begun by
Xenophanes and continued in the dramatists of the Socratic
period—though, as we saw, this leads on the whole, not so
much to atheism as to a refined conception of deity.

Thirdly, we should note the growing tendency to agnosticism which reaches its zenith in the Sceptical schools of late
Antiquity—the feeling that the subject matter of theology is
too complex and human life too short to admit of any firm
conclusions on these matters. This is a mood which will occur
again and again in the history of thought.

Fourthly, it is interesting to note the tendency, on the part of the atheists of this period, to offer a naturalistic account of the origin of religion and religious conceptions. These too will persist and we shall come across this again when we come to look at the nineteenth century.

Lastly, we should pay particular attention to the materialism which we find in the fifth century Atomists for this again will be revived in the nineteenth century and used as an argument in the continuing debate between faith and unbelief.

We thus see that the Classical period, so far as the thinkers and philosophers are concerned, is not one in which a religious understanding of the world has it all its own way. Voices, powerful and insistent voices which will echo down subsequent ages, are raised against the religious way of looking at things. The seeds, and towards the end of the period almost the full flower, of agnosticism and atheism are there.

The closing of the pagan philosophical schools by the Christian Emperor Justinian in AD 529 can be taken as marking the end of the Classical and freethinking period of thought. For almost six hundred years after this thought in the Western World will be dominated by the Christian understanding of reality as that was articulated philosophically under Platonic and neo-Platonic influences. Not until the rise of the Arabian and Jewish philosophers of the eleventh and twelfth centuries will anything resembling the free speculative intelligence of Greece occur, and so without further ado we will pass now to a discussion of belief and unbelief in the Mediaeval period.

Note on Atheism and Agnosticism within Jewish Thought in the period before the Fall of Jerusalem in AD 71

Salis Daiches, writing about atheism within Judaism, has this to say: 'Atheism as a system of thought has no place in Judaism and there is no equivalent for the term in the Hebrew language. . . . The deliberate denial of the existence of a Being who is responsible for the activity of nature and for the course of history presupposes a systematic analysis and explanation of natural and historical phenomena as the necessary effects of existing uncreated causes. The ancient Hebrew had no disposition to analyse the natural phenomena in the way the Greek did and to trace them back to physical laws and principles—the indispensable basis of all conscious atheistic doctrines.'[2] While, as an account of the Hebraic approach to the world, this is true, we should note that ancient Israel was not unacquainted with the phenomenon of unbelief. The writer of Psalm 14 says for instance that 'The fool hath said in his heart, "There is no God".' But on the whole Psalmist and Prophet protest not so much against lack of theoretical belief in God as against a practical atheism which ignores the moral demands of God and acts as if He will not punish unrighteousness.

The only Jewish writer to actually discuss atheism is the first century Alexandrian Jew, Philo, who devotes two chapters of his *De Somniis* to the refutation of atheism—but he, of course, is writing in a very different setting from that of traditional Hebraic culture.

Mention should, however, be made of the mood of extreme pessimism which we find in the later (Greek influenced) Wisdom literature and in the book of *Ecclesiastes* in particular. This is not atheism in the theoretical sense, but again it approaches very close to a practical atheism and agnosticism with regard to the possibility of a relationship with the divine.

NOTES

[1] Rudolf Bultmann, *Jesus and Mythology* p 16
[2] Hastings (edit), *Encyclopaedia of Religion and Ethics* Vol 1 p 187

# PART II

# WESTERN ATHEISM TO THE SEVENTEENTH CENTURY

# SIX

# THE MIDDLE AGES

## The Twelfth and Thirteenth Centuries

TAKEN OVERALL, the four centuries of European history, from the twelfth to the fifteenth centuries, which comprise the Middle Ages, are not without certain similarities to the period at which we have just looked. Professor Dom David Knowles, in his study of the evolution of Mediaeval thought, notes three stages of development common to both the Classical and the Mediaeval periods, and while the comparison must not be pressed too far, it is a useful skeleton to bear in mind. The three factors which Knowles isolates for comparison are firstly at the outset of both periods, a sudden and inexplicable intellectual awakening; secondly, the part played in this awakening by dialectical and speculative philosophy; and thirdly, as at the time of the Sceptics, so towards the end of the fourteenth century, we find the weapons of logic and dialectic turned against venerable institutions and doctrines. 'There too,' he writes, 'a sceptical and opportunist school of thought succeeded in breaking up the fabric constructed by the great creative masters.' [1] There is, however, one important difference between the speculation of Antiquity and that of the Mediaeval period, and one that is highly important as regards the development of thought in a secular direction. It is that in the Greek world free speculation was not unduly hampered by a theocratic form of society, nor by pressure from established ecclesiastical institutions. In the Middle Ages we find many of the more daringly speculative thinkers continually running foul of entrenched and established orthodoxy. The context of thought was the University, which arose in the twelfth century out of the earlier cathedral schools, and which, although

C

employing lay masters, was controlled almost absolutely by the Church and its monastic orders, with all the weapons of suppression at their command. It is not until the breakdown of the Mediaeval social structure of Church and Empire in the fourteenth and fifteenth centuries that we come across the explicit expression of agnostic and atheistic opinion—with perhaps one notable exception, namely the pantheistic school discovered at Paris in the early part of the thirteenth century.

But before turning to look at secular thought, such as it is, during this period, it will be as well for us to give a brief outline of the development of thought from the end of the Classical period.

The period of Christian thought which began in the second century with the Greek and Latin Fathers of the Church is one which is dominated by Plato and neo-Platonic ways of thinking. While Aristotle was not unknown, most of his major works were not available and it is not until the reintroduction of his philosophy in the twelfth century that we find his influence predominating. When, however, he is reintroduced into the Western tradition by way of his Arabian and Jewish commentators, he finally comes to dominate and all but eclipse the older Platonic tradition.

It is in fact the introduction of Aristotle, particularly by way of the Arabian commentators, that brings us to the nearest approach to unbelief in the early Mediaeval period.

Knowles sums up the situation as follows: 'The introduction of the whole canon of Aristotle to the West was a process continuing over a hundred years. The first wave, that of the logical works, was absorbed easily and avidly, for it prolonged and perfected a discipline which was already committed to the Aristotelian mode. The second wave, that of the difficult and profound philosophical works, gave more trouble and was less easily absorbed, though its effects were epoch making. Finally, the ethical and political and literary treatises presented

Europe with a philosopher who regarded human life from a purely naturalistic this-world point of view. Taken as a whole the translations of Aristotle gave Western thinkers, for the first time, matter on which to construct a full and mature system, but the atmosphere, the presuppositions of this great body of thought were not Mediaeval and Christian, but ancient Greek and non-religious, not to say rationalistic in character.'[2]

As we remarked in the previous chapter, God, for Aristotle, was merely, if not wholly, a metaphysical postulate, necessitated by the need to explain change and movement in the world—a conception far removed from that of the living God of Christian Faith. For the rest his system in all its aspects is naturalistic in tone and temper. Furthermore, two other theses, opposed to Christian (and Islamic) doctrine are found in his works—the eternity of the world, and the consequent denial of the act of creation by which Christian (and Islamic) Faith holds that God brought the world into being; and secondly, the denial of anything approaching personal immortality.

Aristotle's Arabian commentators, the most famous and influential of whom were Avicenna (AD 980–1037) and Averroes (AD 1126–98), as they were known to the West,[3] also found great difficulty in reconciling these Aristotelian doctrines with Islamic Faith.

Avicenna, in the early part of the eleventh century, succeeded to a large extent in neo-Platonizing Aristotle and thus made him more acceptable to Islamic doctrine.

Averroes, a century later, seeking as he did to present Aristotle whole and uncorrupted by neo-Platonic thinking, ran into greater difficulty. His way out was to put forward a doctrine of differing degrees or levels of truth—later known as the doctrine of the twofold truth[4]—a doctrine which was to have considerable influence throughout the Mediaeval period and beyond, and which was to influence St Thomas Aquinas' distinction between faith and reason. This doctrine maintained, not, as has sometimes been thought and as many were later to take it, that two contradictory propositions could be true at the same time, but that different minds required truth in different ways. For the simple and unintelligent, faith and authority were sufficient. For the philosopher, absolute demonstration was needed. In effect, as Gordon Leff says, Averroes' doctrine was 'giving a carte blanche to philosophy independent of and in opposition to the tenets of faith'.[5] The doctrine of the twofold truth was to become a convenient tool in the fourteenth century when the conflict between faith and reason became particularly acute.

At the moment, however, our concern is with the influence of Averroën Aristotelianism in the early part of the Mediaeval period. It was not inconsiderable. Writing of it, the great German Mediaevalist Friedrich Heer, in his book *The Mediaeval World*, has this to say. 'Certain teachings acted like a habit forming drug; thus, matter is eternal and perpetually in motion, there has never been any creation in time, there is but one intellect, the power of thought which all men have in common; there is but one world soul subsisting in all living things; there is no personal immortality; faith and knowledge must be kept severely apart; science is concerned only with nature and natural processes and theology is not a science.'[6]

It is in bringing about the situation described in Heer's last three statements, namely the severance of faith and reason, and the view that science is concerned with nature and natural processes and that theology is not a science, that to Averroën influences can properly be ascribed the beginnings of the modern world view and of that secularizing process which was to push theology out of our understanding of the world and confine it within the realm of 'faith'. We shall have more to say about this development when we come to look at the fourteenth century.

For a moment let us note that the reintroduction of Aristotle into European thought resurrected the freethinking speculative intelligence of Greece. Two figures of the late twelfth century stand out: Amaury of Bêne and David of Dinant.

In Amaury of Bêne, whose body was exhumed and burnt in 1210, four years after his death, one can detect, according to Heer, 'the origins of that earth bound humanism which the Averroistic Aristotelians worked out decisively and clearly in the thirteenth century to make it the base for further advances'; and he adds, 'It has been the foundation of militant, non-Christian humanist thinking ever since, right down to Gide, Sartre and Camus.'[7]

We do not know as much as we would perhaps wish about Amaury's opinions, and what we do know, we know at second hand only by citation, but it would appear that he taught among other things that hell is ignorance and that it is within us like a bad tooth; that God is identical with all that is, even evil, and that a man who knows that God works through everything cannot sin and finally; that such a man's recognition puts him in heaven, which is the only possible resurrection. There is no other life and man's fulfilment, therefore, must be in this life alone.

The sources of these doctrines were not only Aristotelian. As Leff points out, the pantheistic proposition that God *was* all things is an easy, if momentous, step from the neo-Platonism of Erigena and the School of Chartres who saw God *in* all things.[8]

The pantheism of David of Dinant, whose name was linked in the conciliar condemnation with that of Amaury, was somewhat different. Heer describes him as an out-and-out Aristotelian and a materialist. Leff calls him a monist. What he appears to have taught is that God is matter and that there is no reality outside God. Matter, thought and God are for him identical.

There we must leave them. Their interest for us is not so much in what they taught—though some of Amaury's views are interesting to say the least—but as examples of a resur-

gence, after about a thousand years, of speculative freethinking
and a refusal to be constrained within the bounds of orthodox
Christian doctrine, when reason dictated otherwise. As the
Middle Ages progress we shall see this tendency coming more
and more to the fore. The sources of such freethinking are to
some extent neo-Platonic, to a greater extent Aristotelian,
but above all their source lies in the indomitable spirit of certain men who refuse to accept anything but what their reason
dictates as acceptable to them. It is a spirit which will grow in
strength as time goes by.

St Thomas Aquinas, in the thirteenth century, stems the
rising tide of secular thinking, more or less successfully, for a
time, both by interpreting Aristotle in such a way as to inte-
grate him into Christian natural theology and by taking up
and developing the now celebrated distinction between faith
and reason.

St Thomas sees no contradiction between the two. There
are some things, such as the existence of God, which can be
proved by natural reason starting from empirically observed
features of the natural world. But he recognizes that the majority of men, having little capacity and time for thought about
these things, will have to accept such truths by faith. There are
other truths, not opposed to reason, but which reason, at least
in its corrupted state, cannot establish and which are known
solely by faith; such for instance is the truth that the world was
created. Faith and reason are not, therefore, opposed. They are
differing and complementary avenues to truth. Occasionally
they overlap—over the existence of God for example; but for
the most part they are separable but not contradictory. Should
reason arrive at a conclusion at variance with revealed truth
St Thomas would take this as a sign that either the thinker's
premises were false or his argument faulty. Faith is, therefore,
supreme—the norm—and reason subject in the last resort to it,
although in certain matters St Thomas does recognize that
philosophy is autonomous. It is this relationship between faith

and reason, theology and philosophy, which will be radically changed in the breakdown of this synthesis which we shall observe in the coming century, where, as we shall see, the tendency was for them to grow further and further apart. Reason, freed from the control of faith, is left to explore the natural world on its own terms and eventually becomes indifferent to anything that faith might have to say.

## The Fourteenth Century

To turn then to the fourteenth century—'The Sceptical Century' as Leff terms it— where secular ways of looking at the world become more firmly established, paving the way for the advancement of naturalistic science in the sixteenth and seventeenth, and above all, in the eighteenth century.

What we see in many of the leading thinkers of this century is the naturalistic approach developed even further and the pantheistic strains, evident in the late twelfth and early thirteenth centuries, dropping out. Any knowledge of God and of his relationship to the world is now affirmed almost entirely on the basis of faith.

The social background of the period should also be noticed. The fourteenth century is one of upheaval in practically all areas of life and thought. Papal and Imperial authority is on the wane and man's confidence in the powers of speculative reason begins to diminish.

According to Leff, in the work to which we have referred, the dominating intellectual interest of the century is not, as was once thought, the debate between realism and nominalism, but a desire on the part of the leading thinkers to disengage faith and reason. 'The distinction between faith and reason,' he writes, 'to which St Thomas so firmly held was taken to make each self-contained; the natural and the supernatural were not merely on different planes but without meeting point; since they dealt with different truths they could not inform one another.'[9] This, as Leff points out, could not but lead to rival outlooks. On the one hand, to a self-contained empiricism, in which fact was the touchstone, and to move beyond which was to enter the realm of uncertainty and conjecture, and on the other, to the belief that matters of faith were not subject to reason—a view that could not but lead to scepticism towards faith on the part of those committed to reason. So far as reason was concerned the rulings of revelation were held to have no validity. Faith too became increasingly independent and looked to revelation and authority for support rather than to rational thought. Once again, in many of the leading thinkers of this period, we see scepticism and authority working hand in hand to uphold traditional orthodoxy.

Copleston in his great *History of Philosophy* confirms these tendencies.[10] He too notes the tendency in Averroën, or 'integral' Aristotelianism as he calls it, to separate faith from reason, theology from philosophy, and to assert the complete independence of each from the other. Once philosophy became recognized as an independent discipline, he says, and he attributes this to a large extent to the fourteenth century interest in logic as against metaphysics, it is only to be expected that it should tend to go its own way and that its subjection to and alliance with theology should disappear—a situation which we find in the movement associated with the name of William of Ockham (*c* 1300–49), although in Ockham himself we also find that alliance of scepticism and authority to which we have referred. Like Sextus Empiricus, Ockham maintains that if reason cannot establish faith, it cannot on the other hand destroy it, and he can thus rest confidently in the status quo. With Pomponazzi, a leading Averroën of the Renaissance, he might well have said, 'I believe as a Christian what I cannot believe as a philosopher'.

Ockham is also a good example of the fact that, as we have said, the important work of the century was that of realigning faith and reason. The question that he asked was of the order, 'How much can reason know of faith?' and his answer, and that of the movement associated with his name, was 'very little'.

This question had also, in fact, been raised and answered in similar fashion during the latter part of the previous century by Duns Scotus (1220–1308) who had also directed his thinking to disengaging what belonged to theology, from what was accessible to reason. In Leff's opinion he led the first general retreat of reason from faith and radically redefined the relationship between them. Two considerations dominated his thinking. The limitation of reason and the absolute freedom of God. His aim, therefore, was to redefine the respective realms of philosophy and theology in such a way as to limit philosophy to a study of Being and its attributes and to leave theology in sole possession of the study of God and his attributes. Reason, he maintained, could not confirm what is revealed by God because the acceptance of revelation is a matter of faith and not of natural experience.[11] The theologian and the philosopher cannot be the same for the subject matter of each is different. Thus theology was excluded from being a science. Though Scotus himself offered a proof of God's existence from 'Being'—one not unlike the ontological argument of Anselm in the eleventh century—in doing so he cut at the two modes of knowing God's existence as hitherto conceived: from sense-experience and from divine illumination. A proof drawn from the physical world could not go beyond the physical world and if proof was to be *a posteriori*, as was generally agreed, there could be no place for divine illumination.

The picture of Duns Scotus as one of the earliest purely fideist thinkers is reinforced if we look at the theological side of his thinking. God, for Duns, is defined primarily in terms of will. God, he says, is pure will, and therefore no explanation can be offered, by reason, of his ways. There is, in Scotus' thinking, a discontinuity between God and the created world, such as had not existed, for instance, in Aquinas. By making God's will the only law of creation, the unknowability of God became Scotus' starting point and the discrepancy between faith and reason established a situation fraught with terrible consequences for theology, for this dichotomy between faith and reason, the supernatural and the natural, established by Scotus within the mainstream of Christian theological thinking, freed reason for the exploration of the natural world on its own restricted terms. As Leff expresses it, 'His system upset the precarious balance between faith and reason. He had breached their unity too far for others not to widen it . . . natural reason could not transcend the limitations of secondary causes. God is unconstrained and therefore faith alone and not reason could describe him.' [12] Leff's final judgment is worth noting. 'The scepticism that came from Scotism,' he says, 'is at the opposite end of the pole from that of Ockhamism but it is scepticism none the less and was Duns' greatest legacy to the fourteenth century.' [13]

The issues which Scotus raised and which were to continue throughout the next century and beyond, were devastating in their consequences for theology and eventually for religion as well; for Scotus, and following him Ockham, were not just separating reason from faith. What it is more important for us to consider is why they felt that reason could have nothing to do with the matters with which faith was concerned. What they questioned was metaphysics as such, and their work displays therefore their radical lack of confidence in the ability of the mind to transcend the natural world and to establish knowledge of that which lies beyond sensory experience—a lack of confidence which as Western thinking developed was to be brought to definitive expression in the eighteenth century in the philosophical writings of Immanuel Kant.

Alternatively, we can see this development as the restricting of what was involved in the very meaning of reason. The early thinkers of the Middle Ages drew a distinction between the understanding as *ratio* and the understanding as *intellectus*.[14] *Ratio* was the power of discursive logical thought; of searching and of examination, of abstraction, of definition, and of the drawing of conclusions. *Intellectus* was the understanding in so far as it has the capacity of *simplex intuitus*—in which truth is apprehended receptively. For St Thomas and the early Middle Ages the faculty of the mind, man's knowledge, is both of these things in one—simultaneously *ratio* and *intellectus*. The process of knowing is the action of the two together.

In the late Middle Ages, with the emphasis on logic, rather than metaphysics, the understanding as *intellectus* gives way to an almost exclusive concentration on the understanding as *ratio* and reason became restricted to the discovery, not any longer of truths about Being, but of the relationships which existed among sensible things.

Relying solely on the answers given by faith men no longer felt the need to ask such questions of reality and so they gradually dropped out of the mainstream of philosophical thinking to be revived only intermittently in the ages to come.

From what we have said so far it will be evident that William of Ockham's positions were well prepared. His achievement was to weld them into 'a devastating unity which for sheer destructive capacity was unequalled during a thousand years of discussion'.[15]

Ockham was primarily a logician, and a logician who criticized metaphysical arguments and proofs in the name of logic. In particular he criticized the alleged demonstrations of the existence of God and of the immortality of the soul on the grounds that either they did not rest on self-evident principles or that the conclusions did not follow from the premises. He admitted, however, that some metaphysical arguments might be probable. Ockham's philosophy combines a thoroughgoing empiricism with an equally radical contingency. For him only the individual thing was real—at least at the immediate point of human experience. For the rest God's will was the arbiter. His thought, therefore, operates at two levels. At the level of the natural he is an empiricist refusing to stretch knowledge be-

yond the bounds of ascertainable experience. At the supernatural level he is at once, like Scotus, both fideist and sceptic
placing all religious certainty on faith and none in reason's
power to establish it.

As Copleston notes, two consequences followed from this.
Theology and philosophy tended to fall apart and philosophy,
the important problems of metaphysics which had served to
link it with theology being relegated to the sphere of faith,
tended to take on more and more a 'lay' character.[16] Ockham,
as Leff points out, gave a new consistency to natural knowledge.

It was left, however, to others in the Ockhamist movement to draw the full sceptical implications from Ockham's
position.

Ockham himself was a theologian preoccupied with freeing
the Christian conception of God from the toils of Greek necessity. With Scotus he was concerned fully to establish the freedom and sovereignty of God. Not so, however, many of those
who followed after him, and whose interests were primarily
philosophical and who seized therefore on the critical side of
his work. Chief among these were Nicholas of Autrecourt and
John of Mirecourt.

Nicholas (c 1300–47) carried the nominalism of Ockham,
with its insistence that only the individual thing is real and that
there is no real connection between things and therefore no
inference from one thing to another possible, to a point not
far short of that which Hume reached in the eighteenth century.
He has in fact been called a mediaeval Hume.[17] He too denied
that we could have any rational knowledge of that which lies
beyond sensory experience. The only certainty that we possess
is confined to logic and mathematics and immediate perception. Theological certainty was not a matter of experience and
reason but rested solely on revelation accepted by faith.

The disengagement of philosophy from theology which we
see in the fourteenth century, and which turned philosophy

away from metaphysical speculation towards an interest and a concern with the world of experience, was reinforced by that upheaval in the whole of Western man's approach to life known as the Renaissance. To this let us now turn.

NOTES

1 David Knowles, *Evolution of Mediaeval Thought* p 83

2 *Op cit* p 192

3 In Arabic, Ibn Sina and Ibn Rushd.

4 Called by some scholars the doctrine of 'double-truth'.

5 Gordon Leff, *Mediaeval Thought* p 157

6 Fredrich Heer, *The Mediaeval World* p 263

7 *Op cit* p 262

8 *Op cit* p 128

9 *Op cit* p 258.

10 Cf Copleston, *History of Philosophy*, Vol 3, Pt 1 p 21

11 Cf the definition of revelation in the *Catholic Encyclopaedia*, where it is defined as 'the communication of some truth by God to a rational creature through means which are beyond the ordinary course of nature'. The Vatican Council of 1870 defined faith as 'a supernatural virtue whereby, inspired and assisted by the grace of God we believe that the things he has revealed are true'. Scotus' use of faith and revelation are very similar, if not identical, with these.

12 Leff, *op cit* p 272

13 *Ibid*

14 For further discussion of this distinction cf Josef Pieper, *Leisure the Basis of Culture* pp 33ff

15 Leff, *op cit* p 279

16 *Op cit* p 23

17 By Hastings Rashdall. See his paper *Nicholas of Autrecourt—a Mediaeval Hume*, P.A.S. 1906–7

# SEVEN

# THE RENAISSANCE AND THE RISE OF SCIENCE

THE PERIOD of intellectual history to which we now turn, and which covers roughly the fifteenth, sixteenth and seventeenth centuries, represents no sudden and complete break with the past. We have seen how, in the late Middle Ages, there was a turning away from theological and metaphysical speculation towards a fuller appreciation and understanding of the natural world, with philosophy taking on more and more of a lay character; and how also, in the Ockhamist movement, logical and scientific interests predominated. Further, as the American scholar Charles Homer Haskins has shown, the Italian Renaissance of the fifteenth and sixteenth centuries was to a large extent determined by an earlier Renaissance in the twelfth century which saw the emergence of vernacular languages, the revival of the Latin classics, poetry and Roman law, the recovery of Greek science and much Greek philosophy, as well as the beginnings of universities, towns and the sovereign state.[1] Most historians of the Renaissance are, in fact, now agreed that almost all of the dominating interests of this period can be found in the late Middle Ages and conversely, that the major movements of the late Mediaeval period continue to grow and develop alongside the renewal of interest in the Classical heritage.

What happened during what we call the Renaissance was that, as Windelband expresses it, 'the undercurrent which for a thousand years had accompanied the religious main movement of the intellectual life among the Western peoples, swelling here and there to a stronger potency, now actually forced its way to the surface'.[2] The result was a readjustment of values and a new way of looking at things. From the point of view of cosmology Copernicus might undermine man's place at the centre of the universe; ideologically the Humanists of the Renaissance placed him and his concerns firmly at the forefront of the picture. Initially, therefore, the change associated with the Renaissance was primarily one of perspective. During this period it began to be borne more and more upon men's minds that this world was worthy of the attention of the best minds, and that man himself, irrespective of whatever supernatural affiliations he might be supposed to have, was not unworthy of study. The Renaissance marks the beginning of that secularized approach to the knowledge of man and his environment with which we today are so familiar. No longer are man and the world seen wholly within the religious context, their place charted and mapped within the hierarchy of Being, a man's actions judged solely in terms of the drama of his salvation, and the world and its contents seen as little more than the outward signs bespeaking inner theological significance. Both man and the world now begin to be approached and understood in and for themselves.

This is not to say, however, that the Italian Renaissance was irreligious, although many historians, particularly during the last century, certainly tended to associate the Renaissance and Italian Humanism with irreligion of one form or another—seeing it as, for example, a secret atheism or as a new Paganism incompatible with Christianity. As one of the leading authorities of this period says, 'The neat separation of reason and faith . . . was considered as a hypocritical device to cover up a secret atheism, whereas the emphasis on a natural religion common to all men found in the work of the Platonists and Stoics was characterized by pantheism.'[3] His own judgment on the early humanism of the Italian Renaissance is quite the opposite of this. 'There was, to be sure,' he admits, 'a good deal of talk about pagan gods and heroes in the literature of the Renaissance, and it was justified by the familiar device of allegory . . . but there were few, if any, thinkers who seriously thought of reviving pagan cults. The word pantheism had not yet been invented, and although the word atheism was generally used in polemics during the late sixteenth century, there were probably very few real atheists and barely a few pantheists during the Renaissance. The best or worst we may say is that there were some thinkers who might be considered . . . as forerunners of eighteenth century freethought.'[4] The real core of the tradition concerning the paganism of the Renaissance is something quite different. It is 'the steady and irresistible growth of non-religious intellectual interests which were not so much opposed to the content of religious doctrine, as rather competing with it for individual and public attention'.[5] This seems to me, so far as the early part of the Renaissance is concerned, to be nearer the truth, although as we shall see it is a judgment which will need some modification as the Renaissance progresses.

The Renaissance falls into two separable but not totally unconnected moments: an earlier aristocratic and Classical Renaissance with its taste for Greek and Roman art and literature and its backward look at what it took to be a Golden Age of humanity—what is often referred to as the Humanist phase of the Renaissance—and a later Renaissance which followed and supplanted it—'a more popular, empirical, less traditional and hierarchical and more scientific and forward looking Renaissance'.[6] The former in many respects prepared the way for the latter. As Windelband says, 'The knowledge of ancient philosophy brought out by the humanist movement was eagerly taken up and the systems of Greek philosophy were revived in violent opposition to the mediaeval tradition. But from the point of view of the whole movement of history this return to antiquity presents itself as but the instinctive preparation for the true work of the modern spirit.'[7] The history of the philosophy of the Renaissance is in the main the history of the process in which the scientific way of understanding the world is gradually worked out from the humanist revival of the Greek spirit.

The early humanistic period is not, however, without interest for us, for it is here that we can detect the beginnings of that sceptical attitude to religion which will become, by the time we reach the eighteenth century, the dominant mood of the Western intellectual tradition. To this let us, therefore, now turn.

### The Classical Renaissance

While the judgment of Kristeller to the effect that during the early humanistic phase of the Renaissance there is very little overt expression of atheistic opinion is by and large true, at least so far as Italy is concerned, it is in fact during this period that the ground is prepared for the more totally secularized approach of subsequent centuries.

That this is so is evident if we look at what was in fact the dominant concern of the humanistic movement—namely the recovering of classical learning. The attitude of the Mediaeval Church to pagan literature was basically one of selection. Some classical authors were on the list of prohibited books *in toto*—as, for instance, were Ovid and Terence—others had only certain of their works on the list, while those which could be reconciled with Christian doctrine were exempt, though the attitude of the Church to such authors as were exempt— Plato and Aristotle for instance—was to regard them not as Pagan at all, but as forerunners of the Gospel and the equal in some respects of the Fathers.

At the Renaissance, due to the devoted scholarly and critical work of the early humanists, classical authors began to be read whole and for their own sake and it was discovered that far from being forerunners of Christianity, they were representative of a culture and way of life complete in itself and in many ways different from and alien to the Christian one.

Buckley, in his study of the atheism of the English Renaissance assesses the situation as follows: 'Since the entire Renaissance tended towards secularism and since the classics began to be understood as the thoughts of an alien religion, it is apparent that a man in sympathy with these movements would find the reading of almost any piece of Greek or Latin literature an experience not likely to make him a sounder Christian. The classics might make him a sounder moralist or a keener philosopher and some might seem superficially to be bolstering up his Christianity, but the event was to show that good moralists and keen philosophers were not always good Christians and that Christianity supported by Pagan thought developed a disconcerting tendency to be neither Pagan nor Christian but a new thing which was known in the course of time as natural religion or deism.'[8]

Further, as he goes on to note, 'Aside from the great body of pure literature, most of which had little religious significance, there was in addition a considerable body of works of a sceptical and enquiring nature—works which had an agnostic if not an atheistic import and which could not be reconciled with the tenets of Christianity.'[9] The influence of these latter, which included Cicero, Plutarch, Pliny and above all Lucian and Lucretius, was not inconsiderable, and, as Buckley in his detailed and well referenced study of the period shows, they form one of the major influences behind French and English freethinking during the fifteenth and sixteenth centuries.

Thus the revival of classical learning worked away from Christianity and to some extent from all religion on two counts. On the one hand it served to turn many thinkers of the period away from a parochial concern with the distinctive claims of one particular religion by introducing them to another and competitive culture—something which was to be reinforced by the travellers and explorers of the period who now began to introduce the West to cultures and civilizations of which they and the Bible which they read were for the most

part ignorant.[10] On the other hand within the newly discovered classical culture itself there was a speculative and
sceptical spirit to which many did not fail to respond.

It is to this, the revival of classical scepticism, that we now
turn. Speaking of England in the sixteenth century, Buckley,
in the study to which we have referred, states that 'it can be
said with confidence that the sceptics of classical antiquity
were one of the major sources for religious doubt'.[11] Pliny,
Lucian, Lucretius, Cicero and Plutarch were read and their
agnosticism and worldly-wise resignation to the human
condition noted and emulated. This is also true of both Italy
and France as well.

Typical of the spirit which the classics helped in no small
wise to create is that which we find in the writings of Miguel
de Montaigne (1533–92), the author of that monument to
ancient scepticism, *The Apology for Raymond Sebond*—later
incorporated into the second volume of his now justly renowned *Essays*. Despairing of knowledge about such compli-
cated issues as the existence of God and the Immortality of
the Soul, yet content to rest in faith in and outward conformity
to the established religion, Montaigne sought peace of mind,
as had Seneca and Plutarch, his favourite authors, before him,
by way of self-knowledge and self-discipline, the twin values
on which, for him, the whole of classical philosophy depended.
As Windelband says, 'Whatever of philosophical thought is
found in the *Essays* arises from Pyrrhonism. Hereby a thread
of tradition which for a long time had been let fall is again
taken up. The relativity of theoretical opinions and ethical
theories, the illusions of the senses, the cleft between subject
and object, the constant change in which both are involved, the
dependence of all the work of intellect upon such doubtful
data—all these arguments of ancient scepticism meet us
here, not in systematic form, but incidentally in connection
with the discussion of individual questions and thus in a much
more impressive manner.'[12]

Sanchez (1562–1632), somewhat later, revived Scepticism in a much more formal philosophic way and looked forward also to a new empirically based science of nature. Charron (1541–1603) too, despairing of theoretical knowledge about the important questions of life, sought in self-knowledge for that practical knowledge which, for him, formed the basis of the moral life.

All three set up the authority of faith and of the Church, however, thus remaining true to the classical sceptical tradition.

But the revival of ancient scepticism was not by any means the only cause of the widespread unbelief which we meet with in the sixteenth century. Other classical authors were equally influential, among them Lucian, whose light scoffing tone appealed to the mood of the time. Lucretius also exercised considerable influence—sufficiently so for Sir Philip Sidney, for example, to devote an entire chapter of his *Arcadia* to his refutation.[13] The Epicureans, as the followers of Lucretius were called, also figure prominently in Calvin's denunciation of atheism in the *Institutes*, where he notes that 'In old times there were some, and in the present day not a few are found who deny the being of God.'—a significant instance of the worry that the growth of unbelief was causing. Linked in Calvin's mind with the Epicureans are the Paduans who, following Averroes, denied the immortality of the soul—a further source of unbelief in the sixteenth century.

Two other sources of unbelief during this period should also be noted.[14] They are firstly, what the age called 'Machievellianism' and secondly, the warfare that was developing between differing Christian denominations. If French and English writers of the period are to be believed, the former represented the greatest single source of atheism in Western Europe. Machiavelli, as Buckley says, was for poets, divines, scholars and pamphleteers alike 'the arch-atheist, the devil who had taught men to use religion for their own ends, who had corrupted France and brought about St Bartholomew's Day, who had taught simple Englishmen to be atheists and who, unless his works were put down or effectively combated, would be the ruin of Christendom. His name Niccolo ("Old Nick") at that time became and has ever since remained a synonym for the devil.' [15] Roger Asham attacked his influence in England in the *Scholemaster* and Gentillet speaking of his influence in France bemoaned and deplored 'the miserie and calamitie of the time wherein wee are, which is so infected with Atheists, and contemners of God and all Religion, that even they which have no religion, are best esteemed, and called in the court language People of service; because being fraughted with all impietie and Atheisme, and having well studied their Machiavel, which they know upon their fingers, they make no scruple or conscience at any thing'. [16]

That the warfare between the innumerable religious sects which flourished in the sixteenth century alongside the warfare of the Roman Catholic church with the newly established Protestant churches should be a cause of unbelief, rather than a witness to widespread religious conviction, is not as strange as it might at first sight appear. For here were a number of bodies, adherents for the most part of the same religion, all claiming an exclusive monopoly of revealed truth. Who was to say, and on what basis, which among them was right? No wonder then that Thomas Nashe in *Pierce Pennilesse* (1592) pointing to the existence of atheists and to the source of their unbelief claimed that religious controversy was the main cause. So also Hooker, who wrote in the *Laws of Ecclesiastical Politie*, that 'with our contentions their (the atheists) irreligious humour is also much strengthened'. [17] Bacon also in his famous essay 'On Atheism' noted such controversies as the first cause of atheism.

Many of the sects themselves were to a large extent agnostic or near atheist, as, for example, were the Unitarians and the Socinians. The latter are of particular interest in that they elevated, and thus anticipated the eighteenth century in this respect, the principle of reason to the status of a supreme first principle and in the history of rationalism theirs would be no mean place. Cheynell, writing in the middle of the seventeenth century and referring to this now firmly established sect, forecast that adherence to this principle would grow.

Buckley says, 'Thinking he was pushing the arguments of the Socinians to the utmost limits of absurdity, Cheynell really delivered a fairly accurate prophecy of what was to take place in the development of philosophical thought during the next hundred years.'[18] Cheynell's words are worth quoting. 'The Socinians lay the principle of reason as their foundation, and keep so close to it that they reject the weightiest articles of the Christian Faith, because reason cannot discover them to be true by her own light, that is reason . . . before the illumination of the Holy Ghost, as they explain themselves. . . . Reason by its own light did discover unto them that the good and great God had prepared eternal happiness for our immortal souls: if this then be enough (as the Socinians say that it is) to receive all things as Principles of Religion which Reason by her own light can discover to be true . . . then the Philosophers, especially the Platonists, were in an happy condition, and it will be lawful for a man to cry out aloud, *Sit anima mea cum Philosophis*, and he shall never be thought an Atheist. . . . Let us then canonize the Heathen for Saints and put Hermes, Phocyledes, Pythagoras, Socrates, Plato, Plotinus, Cicero, Zorcaster, Iamblichus, Epictetus, Simplicius into our Rubricke, and let not Aristotle. Alexander or Averroes be left out.'[19]

Before we turn to the Enlightenment where such thinking as that of the Socinians finds its fulfilment let us look at one other important development which we have so far only mentioned in passing—the rise of science, that second phase of the Renaissance upon which our modern world and its attitudes and beliefs for the most part rest.

*The Rise of Science and the Mechanico–Materialistic Philosophy*

It will be noticed that one often supposed cause of unbelief during this period—the rise of empirical science—has not so far been mentioned. The fact is that while, as was soon to become all too evident, the newly discovered scientific way of understanding the world contained within it the possibility of atheism and unbelief, this conclusion was not explicitly drawn until the seventeenth and the eighteenth centuries. Gabriel Harvey, writing to Edmund Spencer towards the end of the sixteenth century, evinced his annoyance at the tendency of the new science to assign more and more events to natural causes, and many other writers showed themselves more or less aware that science was appropriating to itself an understanding of the workings of the world which had hitherto been within the province of Faith. But Buckley claims that acquaintance with the literature of the sixteenth century yields little if any evidence that agnostics and atheists used arguments drawn from science in support of their case.

He writes, 'One of the most surprising things to a student beginning a study of sixteenth century England is the fact that general writers and the population at large seem to have been unconscious of or not much interested in the revolutionary and era marking discoveries of such pioneers as Magellan and Copernicus. It is not hard to go through the period and pick out quotations from this or that person showing that they knew pretty well what was going on, and certainly the prompt action of the Holy See against Galileo and Bruno shows beyond doubt that those whose interests were most closely concerned were keeping well abreast of the scientific thought of the day. Yet it is none the less true that the new ideas did not rapidly become current and that they did not become subjects for popular controversy until a much later day. There has been much speculation on this point, usually by men who have not burdened their minds with much reading from original sources and it does seem as if the new science should have been an important factor in religious unbelief at least by 1575. But I do not find it to have been so from my readings in the general literature of the period and consequently. . . . I do not regard the scientific discoveries as a major source for religious incredulity in England prior to 1600.'[20] The early scientists themselves certainly drew no such anti-religious conclusions from their work. Francis Bacon, however, in his essay 'On Atheism', written in 1597, lists three types of atheist; the light scoffing type, the atheistical statesman and lastly, the scientific atheist. Unfortunately he says very little about this last class, but that it was in existence by the end of the sixteenth century and continued to increase in the subsequent one until it became a force to be reckoned with in the eighteenth is something of which we should now take note.

One way of looking at the rise of science is to see it as springing from a desire or need for a more satisfying type of explanation. This is the insight which Basil Willey offers us in his penetrating study of the seventeenth century background to English literature. An explanation, for Willey, makes some thing or event intelligible by offering a restatement of it in terms of current interests and assumptions. It satisfies, he says, 'because it appeals to that particular set of assumptions, as superseding those of a past age or a former state of mind'.[21] For an explanation to be satisfying its terms must appear ultimate and incapable of further analysis.

What then were the assumptions which appeared to satisfy the minds of natural scientists in the seventeenth century? What were the assumptions which they superseded and which were felt to be no longer viable? Aristotle had defined four types of causes in terms of which an event or thing might be explained. They were first, the material cause—the substance out of which something was made; secondly, the formal cause

—the idea or model of the thing in mind; thirdly, the efficient cause—that which immediately brings an event or thing into being; and lastly, the final cause—the end or purpose of the event or thing. The interest of the Middle Ages had, until towards their close, centred upon the latter or final cause— the end or purpose of the event or thing, as this was related to the overall purpose of the Creator. Explanation was, therefore, almost exclusively teleological and theological. In the seventeenth century interest (and need) began to shift from the supernatural to the natural understanding of things, from the final to the efficient cause of things, so that events began to be explained not any longer by being set within the context of God's will, but when their natural history had been given.

The changing character of explanation can best be illustrated by reference to comets. To the ancients and to the mediaevals comets were, above everything else, portents, indicative of either the wrath or at least of the will of God. By the time we reach the end of the seventeenth century this explanation is beginning to be superseded, at least in the minds of the educated, by an explanation couched in natural terms. Pierre Bayle (1647–1706), writing of this phenomenon in 1682 attacks the older explanation, endeavouring to show that the belief is fanciful and that no empirical connection can be proved between comets, natural disasters and the will of God. In place of the older theory he substitutes one formulated wholly in natural terms.[22] He goes even further and draws out the implications for theology of such an explanation.

'You are not to believe in the power of comets,' he says (and here I quote from M Paul Hazard's free paraphrase of what Bayle says[23]), 'even if whole nations have borne witness to it, even if millions have sworn to it; nay, even if it be proclaimed by universal consent.' Thus, incidentally, although this is indicative of the spirit of the time, he attacks the major argument used to convince atheists of God's existence. In his own words: 'It is the purest delusion,' he says, 'to suppose that because an idea has been handed down from time immemorial to succeeding generations, it may not be entirely false.' Investigation and not authority is the order of the day, as is the belief in the stability of nature—a stability which does not any longer allow of divine and arbitrary intervention. Bayle, therefore, proceeds to an attack on miracles. Miracles, he argues, are against all reason, for there is nothing more constant with God's infinite greatness than His maintainance of the laws of nature—which He Himself has established. There could be nothing more unworthy than to conceive of Him as interfering with their regular operation. A position which was to become a standard one in the subsequent century, and one which was, perhaps inadvertently, to be a step towards a consistent naturalistic position and which was to push God out of the world into a function not unlike that which He had occupied in the Aristotelian system—of Creator or First Cause. Such a position left the world free for empirical observation unfettered by supernaturalistic assumptions. The world was a rational and self-contained system which, when its existence had been attributed to a once and for all divine creative act, could be understood without any further reference to the supernatural.

It should, however, be pointed out that the newer method of explaining events in the world does not necessarily contradict nor even imply the falsity of the older teleological explanation. Other questions were now being asked and other answers given, arising out of a different way of looking at the world and indicative of different needs. As Willey puts it: 'Speaking generally, it may be said that the demand for explanation is due to the desire to be rid of mystery. Such a demand will be most insistent when the current mysteries have become unusually irksome, as seems to have been the case in Epicurus and again at the Renaissance. At these turning points men wanted "scientific" explanations because they no longer wished to feel as they had been taught to feel about the nature of things. To be rid of fear—fear of the unknown, fear of the gods, fear of the stars, or of the devil— to be released from the necessity of reverencing what was not to be understood; these were amongst the most urgent demands of the modern as of the ancient world; and it was because it satisfied these demands that scientific explanation was received as the revelation of truth.'[24]

But as Willey goes on to point out, 'There was demanded more than the release from traditional hauntings. Men demanded also to feel at home in this brave new world which Columbus, and Copernicus, and Galileo had opened up to them and to recognize it as "controlled, sustained and agitated" by laws in some way akin to those of human reason. To be no longer at the mercy of nature, no longer encompassed by arbitrary mystery—these benefits were to be accompanied by the great new gift of power, power to control natural forces and to turn them, in Bacon's phrase, to "the occasions and uses of life" and the "relief of man's estate".'[25]

This is the beginning of the modern spirit—of what the German theologian Bonhoeffer, who did so much to interpret this spirit to the religious men of our own age, called 'man's coming of age', Prometheus unchained—of which Swinburne in the nineteenth century was to sing 'Glory to man in the highest, for man is the master of things'.

We shall have more to say about this when towards the close of our study we come to look at the philosophical issues involved in the dialogue of belief with unbelief. What it is important for us to notice now is that this new way of looking at and coming to terms with the world was not so much argued as assumed and insinuated. Older ways of regarding phenomena were not overtly shown to be false. They were simply superseded and dropped out of consideration as man's interest and need changed. There are some indications that today western man's interest and need is changing yet again and that he is once more searching for other meanings and other interpretations of the world and of himself than those supplied by science. But more of this later.

To return to the seventeenth century. For some time, until about the middle of the eighteenth century in fact, the differing explanations of religion and science existed side by side. The doctrine of the twofold truth—of the truths of faith and of the truths of reason—safeguarded both supernatural explanation as well as belief in that world behind or above the natural which was still man's other, if not any longer his true, home. With Sir Thomas Browne the majority of seventeenth century thinkers might be described as 'great amphibians', living simultaneously in the natural and the supernatural orders.

Nevertheless, to quote Willey again, 'if a revolution was in process of enactment, it was a general transference of interests from metaphysics to physics, from the contemplation of Being to the observation of Becoming'.[26]—a process which, as we have seen, began in the late Middle Ages. By the end of the seventeenth century it was well nigh complete.

Three philosophers of the seventeenth century stand out and in their differing ways typify this development. They are Descartes (1596–1650), Hobbes (1588–1679) and Spinoza (1632–77). Each in his own way articulates the new philosophy and each is important as illustrating what was now becoming the standard relationship of the new philosophy and religious belief. To turn to Descartes first.

'To the cause of religion, the Cartesian philosophy came bringing what seemed a most valuable support, to begin with. But that same philosophy bore within it a germ of irreligion which time was to bring to light and which acts and works and is made deliberate use of to sap and undermine the foundations of belief.'[27] This judgment of M Paul Hazard on the ultimate significance of Cartesianism for religious belief is one which is echoed by many other historians of ideas.[28] Prima facie it is a strange one, for Descartes himself saw his philosophy as offering religion just that intellectual support which in his opinion it so badly needed. The existence of God was as demonstrably certain for him as the existence of the self or soul. However, as Hazard notes, the hallmark of the Cartesian approach was clarity, examination, inquiry and criticism—and this was no less true of Descartes' approach to religion. Matters which aforetime had been a matter for faith and experience now came perilously close to becoming rational hypotheses, a status which, as time was to show, militated against their being at the same time the objects of religious commitment.[29] This tendency was reinforced when Descartes, having sharply distinguished the soul from the body, invoked God to account for the harmonious working together of these two disparate ontological entities. No wonder that the deeply religious Pascal was to distinguish so passionately between God, the God of Abraham, Isaac and Jacob and the God of the philosophers.

Willey's judgment, which reinforces that of Hazard, to the effect that 'Cartesian thought reinforced the growing disposition to accept the scientific world picture as the only true one' and thus told against the insights of both poetry and religion, which 'spring from quite other modes of knowing',[30] would therefore seem quite justified. God, banished from the realm of living experience to that of rational explanation, had a tendency to disappear altogether when more naturalistic hypotheses came along. The story of Newton, as related by Professor C. A. Coulson, illustrates very well the tendency of the new science to evoke God as a hypothesis at those points where, temporarily as it turned out, scientific explanation failed. He writes: 'Newton, trying to apply his splendid discovery of the law of gravitation to as many different problems as possible, and finding that although it would deal with the motion of the moon round the earth, and the earth round the sun, it would not deal with the spinning of the earth around its polar axis to give us night and day, wrote to the Master of his Cambridge college, Trinity: "the diurnal rotations of the planets could not be derived from gravity, but require a divine arm to impress it upon them".'[31]

Thus was God accommodated to the new scientific way of interpreting events in the world, to be finally banished altogether—or at best relegated to the position of First Cause—when to adapt Laplace's famous words to Napoleon 'there was no further need of that hypothesis'. Such a move was fatal to religion and could not but advance the growth of naturalism.

The fully articulated naturalistic position is best exhibited by the English philosopher Thomas Hobbes—the atheistic implications of whose philosophy were fully appreciated and relished by his contemporaries.

Writing about Hobbes, Richard Peters notes the occasion towards the end of his long life when Hobbes, not for the first time, felt himself to be in mortal danger—and with good cause, for after the Plague and the Great Fire of London, some reason was sought for God's displeasure in bringing about these calamities—the more so on a nation who had so recently been favoured with so great a sign of His goodness towards them as the defeat of the Spanish Armada. 'What more likely,' says Peters, 'than that a people should suffer who gave shelter to a notorious atheist like Thomas Hobbes?'[32] A Bill was brought before parliament for the suppression of atheism and a committee set up to look into Hobbes' major work *Leviathan*. Hobbes himself, however, never openly professed himself an atheist. In fact quite the opposite. His philosophy, however, was avowedly naturalistic and indeed materialistic. 'The universe,' he wrote, 'that is the whole mass of all things that are, is corporeal, that is to say, body, and hath the dimensions of magnitude, namely, length, breadth, and depth; also, every part of body is likewise body, and hath the like dimensions, and consequently every part of the universe is body, and that which is not body is no part of the universe: and because the universe is all, that which is no part of it is nothing, and consequently nowhere.' [33] Quantification with a vengeance indeed! Such an ontology must preclude any and every truck with the supernatural and the transcendent, with anything so immaterial as God—a view which is reinforced if we consider Hobbes' treatment of the soul and of freewill, both of which are described and explained in material terms, although the existence of the latter is denied outright.

Hobbes' explanation of religion, which he comes very near at times to equating with superstition, is no less flattering to that phenomenon. Hobbes, as Peters points out, is one of the few thinkers in the seventeenth century, when religion was still inextricably bound up with everything else, to stand back and attempt in an abstract way to reflect on current religious assumptions. Not only did he rigidly separate theology and religion from philosophy—this in itself as we have seen would be no new thing—but he went further and attempted to offer a naturalistic account of religion in terms which today would be called psychological. Religion, he says, arises out of man's curiosity; out of his desire to know (or invent) the causes of things, especially of good and evil fortune, as well as out of his fear of the unknown. He writes, '(In four things) consisteth the natural seed of religion: opinion of ghosts, ignorance of second causes, devotion towards what men fear, and taking of things casual for prognostics.' [34] To some extent a man's religion is a tribute to his innate, if misplaced, rationality, his sense of order and his desire for meaning. But the difficulty with evoking supernatural causation to account for happenings within the world is, as we have seen with reference to Newton, that it has an uncanny propensity to become supernumerary as naturalistic explanation advances. Hobbes, however, having offered the above explanation of religion is too good a philosopher to accept that he has thus explained religion away. He goes on to distinguish what he calls 'true religion' from 'superstition'. But the criterion which he uses to distinguish these two things is not as clear as we might wish. In chapter 45 of *Leviathan* he writes, 'Fear of power invisible, feigned by the mind, or imagined from tales publicly allowed, RELIGION: not allowed SUPERSTITION. And when the power imagined is truly such as we imagine, TRUE RELIGION.' The difficulty here is knowing just what Hobbes means by 'truly' as against 'falsely imagine', for Hobbes elsewhere maintains that truth can only be significantly affirmed of propositions and not of the products of our imagination.

The only conclusion that we can draw is that, for Hobbes, religious beliefs were not such as to be true or false but were rather expressions of devotion resting on our faith in the person propounding them.[35] This view is reinforced by what Hobbes says about religious belief elsewhere. Religion for him is almost wholly a matter of faith. It is also useful and necessary as an instrument of social order. Hobbes did, however, hold that God was the cause of the world and he offers in *Leviathan* a fairly standard version of the Cosmological Argument.[36] Apart however from the assertion of the existence of God there is nothing else on the basis of natural reason that can be asserted of God's nature. The superlatives that men have used to describe the nature of God—most high, holy, supremely good, etc—are simply expressions of our admiration. Our only other recourse is to describe God negatively by means of such adjectives as infinite and incomprehensible, and to rely on revelation as interpreted by the sovereign. The reverence which we owe to scripture as the vehicle of God's word is in the last resort simply another aspect of our general obligation to obey duly constituted authority.[37]

Our final verdict, therefore, must be that while Hobbes is not strictly speaking an atheist, he is not really a religious man either. Religion he believes is necessary to the well-being of the Commonwealth. It is a matter for obedience and faith. The irony of his final judgment on religion is matched, as Willey says, only by the concluding paragraphs of Hume's essay on miracles. 'For it is with the mysteries of our religion,' he says, 'as with wholesome pills for the sick, which, swallowed whole, have the virtue to cure; but chewed, are for the most part cast up again without effect.'[38]

Spinoza's position is much more sophisticated. Though of a more inherently religious temper than Hobbes, his presuppositions are very much those of the new philosophy of the seventeenth century and while his model of the way in which the world works is derived more from mathematics and logic than from mechanics, his universe is no less rigidly deterministic than is that of Hobbes, except that for cause and effect his more metaphysical mind substitutes ground and consequent. For Spinoza God is the ground of the world; theologically he is a pantheist. God, for him, is no metaphysical or quasi-scientific postulate standing outside the natural order in the relationship of First Mover. He is the natural order. God and nature (*Deus sive Natura*) for him are identical.

In this sense and in this sense only Spinoza is an atheist. He denies God's transcendence. For the rest his system begins, continues and ends in God. In terms of God all else is seen. God is the only self-existing substance, constituted by an infinite number of attributes of which each expresses an eternal and infinite essence. All that is, is God, and nothing can be or can be conceived apart from Him. All the particulars of our experience, even we ourselves, are modes of His Being. It would be a mistake, however, to see in this just so much mysticism, for the essential point that Spinoza is making concerns the nature of causation—of the way in which the world works; and in his own mind at least this was the outcome of exact definition and rigorous logic. The vulgar distinction between God and the world, the Creator and the created, is for Spinoza the result of the interference of the anthropomorphic imagination rather than of reason. Rid ourselves of all figurative descriptions and images with regard to the word 'God' and reason must lead us to see that God and nature cannot be distinguished. The traditional Judæo-Christian and Aristotelian conception—in which God is imagined as a super-person with a will and purpose akin to that of men, is for Spinoza a conception which involves the theologian in perennial contradictions—over the problem of evil, God's freedom of choice etc. The traditional concept of God is, for Spinoza, a contradictory one.

In place of the traditional and imaginative conception of God's relationship to the world Spinoza postulates one self-dependent substance, that is, one ultimate subject all of whose attributes or modifications are explicable in terms of its own nature—and this he identifies with nature conceived as a whole. This unique, self-determining and all-inclusive substance cannot, by definition, be created by anything outside of itself. The idea of a creator other than nature is therefore contradictory.

Should Spinoza's monistic argument be challenged, his reply is to point to the antinomies which the distinction between creator and creation necessarily involve. One such is as follows: If God is distinguished from nature, which He creates, then God cannot be infinite and all powerful, because there exists something other than Him, which possesses attributes which He does not possess, and which must limit, therefore, His power and perfection.[39] Such a God is inconceivable.

God, then, for Spinoza is not the transcendent but the immanent and eternal cause of things, which, as Stuart Hampshire says in his well-known study of that philosopher, is, once Spinoza's identification of God and Nature has been grasped, simply 'another way of saying that everything must be explained as belonging to the single and all-inclusive system which is Nature, and no cause (not even a First Cause) can be conceived as somehow outside or independent of the order of Nature.'[40]

In thus denying at one and the same time both the notion of a transcendent First Cause and the mechanico-materialistic model of the workings of the universe, Spinoza was striking at the roots of the compromise between faith and reason, theology and science, which was not only operative in his own day but which was to lie at the heart of the Deist compromise of the next century.

Before leaving Spinoza we must say something about his description of the good life as 'the intellectual love of God'. Here again subsequent thinkers, Coleridge and Shelley for instance, were to read mystical significance into a phrase where no such significance was intended—as is evident from proposition XXIV in part V of the *Ethics* where its meaning is simply and straightforwardly explained. The proposition reads: 'The more we understand individual things, the more we understand God.' As Hampshire says, 'To understand God must mean to understand Nature, self-creating and self-created; at the third and highest level of intuitive knowledge every individual detail of the natural world is shown as related to the whole structure of Nature; the more we take pleasure, as philosophical naturalists, in tracing in detail the order of natural causes, the more we can be said to have an intellectual love of God.'[41]

Thus we come to an end of our survey of the dialogue of belief with unbelief in the seventeenth century. By the end of that century the issues are pretty clearly discernible. 'The champions of Reason and the champions of Religion were,' in the words of Pierre Bayle, 'fighting desperately for the possession of men's souls, confronting each other in a contest at which the whole of thoughtful Europe was looking on.'[42] It was a battle which was to continue into the Enlightenment.

NOTES

1 Charles Homer Haskins, *The Renaissance of the Twelfth Century.*

2 Wilhelm Windelband, *History of Philosophy.* Vol II, p 348

3 P. O. Kristeller, *Renaissance Thought* p 71

4 *Ibid* pp 71–2

5 *Ibid* p 72

6 J. Bronowski and B. Mazlish, *The Western Intellectual Tradition* p 23

7 *Op cit* p 351

8 George T. Buckley, *Atheism in the English Renaissance* p 3

9 *Ibid* p 23

10 The full impact of the comparative awareness of other cultures and religions was to be felt most keenly towards the end of the seventeenth century. Cf P. Hazard, *The European Mind 1680–1715,* Chapt 1

11 *Op cit* p 4

12 *Op cit* p 362

13 Sir Philip Sidney, *Arcadia,* Bk III, Chapt X

14 Cf Buckley, *op cit* Chapters III and IV

15 *Op cit* p 31

16 Quoted Buckley, *op cit* p 41

17 Bk V, Sect II, Quoted Buckley p 44

18 *Op cit* p 60

19 Quoted Buckley, *op cit* pp 59–60

20 Buckley, *op cit* p 79

21 Basil Willey, *The Seventeenth Century Background* p 10

22 Letter to MLADC, Doctor of the Sorbonne. 'Wherein it is proved in the light of various arguments derived from Philosophy and Theology that comets are in no sense portents of disaster.' Quoted P. Hazard, *op cit* p 186f.

23 *Ibid* p 188

24 *Op cit* p 12

25 *Op cit* p 13

26 *Op cit* p 13

27 Paul Hazard, *op cit* p 160

28 eg Basil Willey, *op cit* Chapt 5

29 For the further explication of this theme in contemporary philosphy of religion cf Alasdair MacIntyre's essay 'The Logical Status of Religious Belief' in *Metaphysical Beliefs* Ed MacIntyre.

30 *Op cit* p 83

31 C. A. Coulson, *Science and Christian Belief* pp 32–3. It has been brought to my attention, since writing this passage, that it could be rather misleading. Newton's main purpose is to show that the present constitution of the universe could not have arisen by the action of gravity alone out of an initially uniform distribution of matter. To this end he uses several arguments besides the one that has been alluded to.

32 Richard Peters, *Hobbes* p 41

33 Hobbes, *Leviathan* Chapt 46
34 *Op cit* Chapt 12
35 So R. S. Peters, *Hobbes* p 244
36 *Leviathan* 95–6
37 Cf Willey, *op cit* p 109
38 *Leviathan* Chapt 32
39 Spinoza *Ethics* Pt 1, Prop IV.
40 Stuart Hampshire, *Spinoza* p 44
41 *Op cit* p 169
42 Paul Hazard, *op cit* p 9

# PART III

# MODERN ATHEISM

# EIGHT

# THE ENLIGHTENMENT

'MAN COME OF AGE.' This, as we have had occasion to mention, is the description which the German theologian Dietrich Bonhoeffer, who was so tragically killed by the Nazi SS towards the end of World War II, used to describe the modern spirit. It was, however, originally the answer given by Kant when, towards the end of the eighteenth century, he sought to reflect on the meaning of that century and of the term which it had used to describe itself—*Aufklärung*, Enlightenment. His answer to the question, *Was ist Aufklärung?* was that it marked the growing up stage in man's development, his determination to put away childish things, to stand upon his own two feet, to be no longer under tutelage, and above all, to use his reason and to think for himself. The eighteenth century is, *par excellence*, the Age of Reason. If the seventeenth century was the century when the battle between scientific truth and other kinds of truth was fought out, to the detriment of all but scientific truth, the eighteenth is the century when the outcome of that battle is felt in all spheres of life; when the attempt is made to bring not only outward but all other forms of nature, and above all human nature, under the sovereignty of reason and of the scientific model. Man's law, his morality, his art, and his religion as well as society itself, will, it is hoped, be established once and for all on a rational scientific basis, or what was for the eighteenth century virtually the same thing, according to nature. Reason, Law, Nature. These are the pivotal concepts for any understanding of the Enlightenment. The new philosophy of the sixteenth and seventeenth centuries had shown nature working according to Law and had thus established the science of nature. Why should not

society, morality and indeed religion be not similarly established? Begone authority and superstition. As Voltaire (1694–
1778) was to write, 'It is certain that knowledge of nature, the
sceptical attitude towards old fables dignified by the name of
history, a healthy metaphysic freed from the absurdity of the
schools are the fruits of that century when reason was perfected.'

What did all this mean for religion? Scepticism with regard
to the religious world view was, as we have seen, no new
thing. Pierre Bayle had, towards the close of the previous
century, in the words of M Hazard, 'with unflagging persistence advanced his ultimate solution which leads to the
conclusion that nothing can be known beyond all doubt'.[1] He
had also in his essay on 'Comets', to which we have referred,
advanced the view 'that it is only a common prejudice that
induces us to believe that atheism is a most fearful state'.
And Bayle was no spent force as M Hazard shows us in his
study of *European Thought in the Eighteenth Century*.[2] The
*Bibliotèque Germanique*, published in 1729, stated that it was
notorious that 'the works of M Bayle have unsettled a large
number of readers and cast doubt on some of the most widely
accepted principles of morality and religion'. To refute him
was regarded as an act of piety and the attacks on him were as
virulent three-quarters of a century after his death as ever they
had been in his lifetime. In the annals of scepticism few can
equal his influence. His disciples in the eighteenth century
enlarged his attack on religion, taking up his themes that
religion and truth were irreconcilable and that there was no
necessary connection between religion and morality. Voltaire
resurrected his *reductio ad absurdum* argument that what could
not be explained by reason should be explained by religion,
no matter how absurd, and might therefore be claimed a
respectable article of faith.

Bayle's influence waned, however, towards the latter
part of the century for by then many of the positions which
he had taken up were commonplace and the spirits of that

time were more concerned to build than to knock down. The battle was over. Orthodoxy in all but rout. Those who were not out and out atheists had abandoned faith and rested what little religion they had on reason. Where revelation was admitted it too was accommodated to reason.

If unbelief in the seventeenth century was 'veiled and subdued and so to speak tempered by a lingering reverence for Christianity'[3] that of the eighteenth is open and pronounced as well as in large part antagonistic to both the Christian and indeed all religion. Little attempt is made in fact to differentiate the two. This was also the case as we shall see later of the protagonists of religion. Religion according to nature looked for that which was common to all religions. It could not be concerned with the particular claims of any one religion.

Of the conflict between reason and religion in the eighteenth century M Hazard has written that it began as a criticism of the existing social order but that soon the opponents of religion 'openly preferred a charge the like of which for sheer audacity had never before been heard of. Now the culprit was dragged into court, and behold, the culprit was Christ! It was more than a reformation the eighteenth century demanded, it was the total overthrow of the Cross, the utter repudiation of the belief that man had ever received a direct communication from God, in other words, in Revelation. What the critics were determined to destroy was the religious interpretation of life.'[4]

In its place would be set reason and nature—and a moral law unfettered by theology. This, claims Hazard, was the *cause célèbre* of the time and the central issues clear and open. God and the soul or not? This was the question everywhere and upon all lips.

The criticism of religion was also a moral one. While there were those who accepted what Willey has called a 'metaphysical optimism'[5] and who attempted, like Leibnitz (1646–1716), to justify the existing order as 'the best of all possible worlds', there were also those who argued that if theism were true then the universe was little better than a cruel joke. Such was the renegade priest Jean Meslier, curé of Etrepigny in Champagne, who died in 1729, leaving behind him a testament not only to his atheism but to his bitter hatred of religion as the source of all the troubles of mankind and the perpetrator of its cruellest joke. He it was who said that the ills which beset men would not be cured until 'the last king has been strangled in the entrails of the last priest'. Initially he was not an atheist at all but a blasphemer. In his cooler moments, however, he realized that the monster-God that he railed against could not in fact exist—a fact which saddened and depressed him as it would appear later to have saddened and depressed John Stuart Mill and Bertrand Russell, taking the sting out of their rebellious stand. Promethean defiance was not something that accorded well with reason. It was, however, to become a fairly standard attitude in the romantic atheism of the next century.

Eighteenth century criticism, however, while it included a moral criticism, was for the most part naturalistic and was centred on the idea of revelation.

Whereas, as we have seen, previous ages in coming to terms with naturalism had founded its belief upon the doctrine of the two-fold truth—revelation and faith on the one hand and knowledge on the other—the eighteenth century would have no such dichotomy. Religion which could not be established by reason was no religion at all—it was superstition. In this freethinkers, and for the most part theologians also, were united.

The opponents of revelation sought to establish two points: to show that not only in principle could there be no such thing as revelation, but that also, in point of historical fact, there had been no such thing. The former was to them almost self-evident in that revelation partook of the order of the miraculous and, as reason in the form of the scientific philosophy had shown, miracles did not occur. The latter was established by pointing to the untrustworthiness of the record.

Such was the two-fold argument against revelation that could be heard all over Europe, not least in England. Toland, Collins, Thomas Gordon, Wolston, Middleton, Tindal, Thomas Chubb, Thomas Morgan and Peter Annet, to name only a few, were all united in this. Not all, however, were atheists. Toland in his book, *Christianity Not Mysterious* and Tindal in his book, *Christianity As Old As The Creation*, had both sought to establish a purely moralistic form of the Christian religion divorced from revelation and resting upon the basis of natural reason and natural law. They were united with the freethinkers, however, in attacking revelation. Tindal's argument is the most interesting and was due to be repeated when, towards the middle and end of the century, English freethinking spread to France and more particularly to Germany. Religion, he argued, must be based upon the moral law and God subject to it, for if God does not conform to the moral law then He acts simply from caprice—which is unthinkable. If, on the other hand, God does conform to the moral law then there is no need of revelation since man by the light of natural reason can discover this law and recognize his duty to conform to it.

The greatest of the French freethinkers is of course Voltaire. He too, like Toland and Tindal, was not an atheist but a deist and much influenced by the English deists as well as by Newtonian philosophy. His more extreme critics were heard to remark, 'Voltaire is a bigot, he believes in God'. His target—the target of his, on the whole, light but penetrating satire and irony—was not as is often thought, theism as such, nor religion, nor even, except in its most orthodox and institutionalized forms, Christianity, but what has been termed 'persecuting privileged orthodoxy'.

Voltaire's deism is typical of the early part of the century—particularly as this reflected the scientific views of the time. Voltaire, as we have said, was a follower of Newton and

Newtonian physics had all but replaced the Cartesian world view, certainly in England, and also throughout Europe. In this it was aided by new advances in biology, which, as far back as the latter part of the seventeenth century, were beginning to cast doubts on the mechanism and materialism implicit in Cartesian dualism. Both sciences cast doubt on Descartes' deductive method—his attempt to deduce the organization of the world from first principles—and on his notion of clear and distinct perceptions. Both, by first-hand experiments, had shown the world to be other than the Cartesian philosophy claimed it must be, and this had far reaching implications. 'For Descartes, as for almost everyone in the seventeenth century, science, theology and metaphysics were inseparable ways of looking at a unified human experience.

Cartesian philosophy had assumed that men were endowed with the knowledge of certain basic principles whose authenticity was guaranteed by God. By the application of logical argument to these given truths it was possible to arrive at a certain understanding of the world of experience, to discover, not merely scientific laws, but the reason why they were necessary. Locke . . . had discredited the entire concept of innate ideas, for which he had substituted merely human sense-impressions. The new scientist, in his turn, used experiment as his starting point, and not, as Descartes had done, to confirm the product of deductive reasoning. The result was, or seemed to be, the removal of final causes beyond the cognizance of man, whose realm was henceforth circumscribed to laws, without hope of attaining to the reasons behind them.'[6] All knowledge was now felt to be relative to the sense-perception of man and therefore subjective. How things were in themselves and what their relationship was to the Whole and to God were inscrutable—a view echoed by Condillac in his *Traite des Sensations* (1754) and by Réaumur and Voltaire. All 'systems' were suspect. But the replacement of the Cartesian by the Newtonian world view involved more than the abandonment of the search for the causes of causes. As we have remarked in a previous section[7] the Newtonian universe required not just an act of Creation but continuing divine intervention to set it to rights. Whereas the Cartesian philosophy had tended towards a mechanistic view of the physical universe, the Newtonian stressed the impossibility of man's attaining to a knowledge of final causes and the dependence of the world on divine regulation. It was this that appealed to Voltaire and the English deists, and it was this that they urged against the atheists, who, as Voltaire said, had been misled by the Cartesians. In their argument they were aided by those, such as the abbé Pluche, who saw the hand of God as a beneficent Providence everywhere at work ordering nature for the delight and comfort of man.

This, as Hampson has noted, diverted attention away for a time from the more materialistically minded of Descartes' followers, such as Hobbes had been, so much so that 'scientists seemed to have relegated atheism to the lumber room of discarded classical speculation'.[8] Atheism was, however, to be revived and from the middle of the century was to grow and flourish as never before. Let us therefore turn now to those whose thought ran in a wholly secular direction and who advanced and consolidated the naturalistic approach that it is our chief concern to chart.

The situation at about the middle of the century is summed up by Hampson as follows: 'The truce between science and religion, despite the warnings of the French Jansenists in their clandestine publication, the *Nouvelles Ecclesiastiques*, encouraged all to participate in the search for knowledge. The scientists, abandoning the quest for metaphysical implications, were in the main content, like Réaumur, to observe and record. Their findings were acclaimed by the divines as grist for the mills of Providence. Protestant, Catholic and Deist shared a common attitude to experience, as the Christians turned their attention away from original sin and the Deists agreed that the heavens declared the glory of God. In this atmosphere there began the intensive prosecution of scientific research and its emancipation from theological control, that have continued ever since.'[9]

But the static world of the mid-eighteenth century scientists, begun by a single act of divine creation which had established the terrestrial landscape and fixed the species of plants and animals pretty much as they were and which so impressed Voltaire as a mark of divine providence was not destined to survive long. Already by 1764 Voltaire is replying to those, who, with the ancient Atomists, were maintaining that, given infinite time, matter and motion would produce every possible combination of phenomena including the existing one—an argument that we find the sceptically minded Philo putting forward in Hume's dramatic *Dialogues on Natural Religion*. (1779)—and Voltaire is on the defensive.

The period from 1740 onwards witnesses the rise of new scientific ideas which begin to cast doubt on the immutability of the natural order and of the beneficent providence. With little else to support it eighteenth century theism was in danger of collapsing. It would be left to the next century to seek to establish theism on different foundations.

A number of scientific discoveries combined to cast doubt on the basic presuppositions of the early eighteenth century world view. Foremost among them was the changing biological picture of the world. The abandonment of the old genetic doctrine of pre-existence, whereby heredity had been explained according to the theory that the seed of all living creatures had been created at the beginning of the world and simply handed on in procreation, in favour of a theory of spontaneous generation meant the attribution to matter of a form of life and implied that the spontaneous arrangement of matter could provide sentient and intelligent beings. As Buffon wrote: 'Life and movement, instead of being a metaphysical degree of existence, are physical properties of matter.' The theory also removed the necessity for assuming the fixity of the species. The stability of a divinely created and unchanging order was now challenged by a new conception of life as a constant and shapeless flux.

The other major challenge was to the Newtonian assumption of divine intervention. D'Alembert, for instance, argued that the conservation of motion might be explained without evoking such intervention. Irregularities which Newton had assumed to be cumulative were shown to be periodical and self-correcting—a significant example of a naturalistic solution to a problem found by situating it within the context of time. The great age of geology, which was to burst upon the next century, was to reinforce this point. But already doubts were being cast on the Biblical time scale. Science thus began to dispense with God as a necessary factor in its explanation of the universe. The naturalistic advance had begun in earnest and reflective minds were not slow in drawing atheistical conclusions. Chief among those who did so were Diderot (1713–84) and the Baron D'Holbach (1723–89).

Diderot, who collaborated with D'Alembert to produce that monument of eighteenth century thought, *The Encyclopaedia*, was an avowed atheist who utilized the arguments of science in its service. In his book, *Interpretation de la Nature* (1754), for instance, he observed that if gravitation were inherent in matter then chaos was impossible since matter would automatically arrange itself in an ordered way—an argument which Hume was to repeat with modification in his *Dialogues*, and which the most notorious atheist of the day, the Baron D'Holbach, was to develop in a more modern direction. In nature, he was to argue, there is in fact no order or disorder, but only what must appear to us to be so. We call 'disorder' that which disturbs us or afflicts us, but all is order in that all occurs by fixed causation. Kant was to express Holbach's point later in its definitive form by arguing that such is the metaphysical constitution of our minds that we cannot but order the world in the way that we do.

But to return briefly to Diderot, of whom it was said that he was a deist in the country and an atheist in Paris. Diderot also was to revive the old Lucretian argument that the order found in nature might be accounted for by the innumerable chances arising out of the manifold motion of its parts from all eternity having led at length to the present combination. He began as a deist, but soon went beyond that into atheism. If you don't believe in the gods, he said, why just banish them to the intermundane spaces? Why not deny them outright? And this is what he did. He became an atheist, believing that all would be well with the world if only the idea of God could be obliterated. As Hazard says, 'Towards God he was filled with wrath, bitterness and rage; witness his story about the misanthropist who hid himself in a cave and meditated long and deeply as to how he should take vengeance on the human race. At length he came out of his cave shouting loudly God! God! "His voice resounded from pole to pole, and behold, men fell to quarrelling, hating, and cutting one anothers' throats. And they have been doing the same thing ever since that abominable name was pronounced and they will go on doing it till the process of the ages is accomplished." '[10]

It is with the Baron D'Holbach, however, that the truly atheistic tendencies of eighteenth century thought are brought to a philosophical articulation which anticipates the naturalistic argument of the next century. It was at his table that David Hume professed that he had never met an atheist, to be told that he was in the company of seventeen![10] D'Holbach is probably the first unequivocally professed atheist in the Western Tradition. In him we see the logical consequences of the assumptions of the new scientific philosophy brought to their first explicit conclusion, and thus in him we can see what 'Nature' means when divested of all religious associations.[12] Nature or the Universe, for D'Holbach, consists only of matter and motion. Matter, however, is not to be thought of as inert and incapable of motion unless moved from without, for it is eternally in motion. It is also completely determined—as is man, who is equally of course part of nature—a conclusion echoed by that other French atheist La Mettrie in his book, *L'Homme Machine*.

D'Holbach's attack on religion is overt and explicit and can be found in his book, *The System of Nature* (1770). Religion is indicted on three counts: That it offers a wrong basis for morality. Here he anticipates an argument that has found favour in our own century—namely, that it is dangerous to build morality on religious foundations in that should those foundations collapse morality is in danger of collapsing with it. His second criticism is that religion is unscientific and its teachings contrary to scientific truth. And lastly, that it is the mainstay of a corrupt social order, and (and here he anticipates Marx's criticism) with its doctrine of life after death, religion diverts attention away from present evils.

He also offers a naturalistic account of the origin of religion as arising from fear and ignorance—fear of the unknown and ignorance of natural causes. In his argument against the English theologian Samuel Clarke, whose treatise on *The Being and Attributes of God* was a standard work of Christian apologetics at that time, D'Holbach maintains, this time anticipating Marx's precursor Feuerbach, that all that Clarke says of God can be more truly ascribed to Nature, who is truly eternal, infinite and unique. He condemns, however, Spinozan pantheism. A parallel development has taken place in our own time with regard to the dualism of soul and body. God and the soul, as Dr Ramsey, Bishop of Durham, maintains, are 'logical kinsmen',[13] and it is not surprising, therefore, that the conflation of the dualism of God and the World should be followed by a conflation of Soul and Body. But to return to D'Holbach. Nature, for him, is its own end and it has no other aim than to be. He will have no truck with

teleology. But what of morality? This is D'Holbach's primary concern and he seeks to establish morality on other
and firmer foundations than those hitherto provided by religion. The basis of morality, for him, is social and is founded
in our feelings of self-respect. He writes: 'It is asked, what
motives an atheist can have to do good. The motive to please
himself and his fellow creatures; to live happily and peaceably;
to gain the affection and esteem of men, whose existence is
much more certain, and whose dispositions are much better
known, than those of a being by nature unknowable. "Can he
who fears not the gods, fear anything?" He can fear men; he
can fear contempt, dishonour, the punishment of the laws;
and he can fear himself, and the remorse felt by all those who
are conscious of having incurred or merited the hatred of their
fellow creatures . . .'[14] Religion's own record in the moral
field, argues D'Holbach, is far from being meritorious—an
observation which offers him great scope and which he does
not fail to utilize. On the other hand he points to those
atheists—Epicurus, Lucretius, Bodin, Spinoza and Hobbes—
who were peaceable and studious men. 'Hobbes did not
cause bloodshed in England,' he writes, 'where in his lifetime religious fanaticism put a king to death on the scaffold.'[15]
Atheism is not, however, a creed for the people, or at least
not yet, so we need not fear. As an enlightened author, he
claims he is writing for posterity and not for his own times
for whom his atheistical doctrines are too advanced. When
we come to look at nineteenth century atheism in the next
chapter, and to consider Nietzsche's forebodings concerning
the moral consequences of atheism, it will be worth recalling
D'Holbach's eighteenth century optimism.

Two other eighteenth century thinkers, the one Scottish,
the other German but of Scottish descent, must be looked at
if we are fully to understand the development of Naturalism
and its argument with religion at the present time. These are
David Hume (1711–76) and Immanuel Kant (1724–1804).

Hume is a sceptic in the Classical tradition. His influence at the present time is considerable and the 'revolution' that has taken place in philosophy during the present century looks back to him as its originator.[16] He is first and foremost an empiricist in that he holds, with his precursor Locke, that all our knowledge originates in sensation. Impressions and their ideas are the basic postulates of his epistemology. Unlike Locke, however, he admits of no avenue by which religious knowledge might be obtained. He accepts the assumption of his century that belief in God is a rationally provable hypothesis, but holds that such a hypothesis is non-proven. His writings on religion are numerous, but come to mature expression in his *Dialogues Concerning Natural Religion*.

The thesis of this work is difficult to establish, but Professor Norman Kemp Smith, in his study of Hume and his relationship to the *Dialogues*, shows beyond reasonable doubt that the position taken by Philo in the dramatic exchanges of the *Dialogues*, which is that of the sceptic, is nearest to Hume's own position, as established from his other writings, and from those who knew him.[17] In the *Dialogues* Philo reviews all the traditional arguments for the existence of God, including that mainstay of eighteenth century apologetic, the Argument from Design, and endeavours to show that their conclusion is not established. His own untypical eighteenth century conclusion is that the only recourse must therefore be to faith, which, as we have seen, is the conclusion of Classical scepticism. That this for Hume was something that he took seriously, if not perhaps deeply, is attested by the way in which he stood out against the outright atheism which he found rampant in Paris—at the cost of being ridiculed for his 'prejudices'—and by the remark which he is reputed to have uttered amidst the grief and shock of his mother's death in reply to the charge of having abandoned the Christian Faith: 'Though I throw out my speculations to entertain the learned and metaphysical world, yet in other things I do not think so differently from the rest of the world.'[18]

To go in detail into Hume's actual arguments against the rationality of theism would take us far beyond the confines of this book. Two or three, however, stand out. First Hume's analysis of causality and the bearing which this has on the Cosmological Argument for God's existence; secondly, his critique of teleology and the Argument from Design, and lastly, his argument against miracles.

The Cosmological Argument in its classical formulation, as the first of St Thomas' Five Ways, had argued that in order to break the chain of an infinite regress of causal agents we must postulate a first uncaused cause of the world. The argument of course requires the further premise, taken until Hume as self-evident, that every event has a cause. Hume, however, analyses causality empirically in terms of what he calls 'constant conjunction'. To say that A causes B is to say no more than that whenever we have observed A we have seen that it is followed by B and vice versa. We can therefore reasonably predict that whenever we observe A it will be followed by B, and conversely, that whenever we observe B, that A has preceded it. Causality is a relationship between two observables. Therefore neither God, nor the world, nor the relationship between them, being observable, Hume concludes that we cannot speak of God as the ultimate cause of the world. To do so we would have had to observe worlds coming into being and to have also observed that no world came into being without the agency of a God. It ought perhaps to be said that this argument is only valid against the causal formulation of the Cosmological Argument and not against some of its other and more recent formulations.[19] But in the eighteenth century the causal form was by and large its only form and Hume's point was on that account well aimed.

Hume's criticism of the Argument from Design was even more telling. This argument, known also as the Teleological

Argument, sought to argue from the appearance of order in the world, from the 'adaptation of means to ends', to a divine Designer. It was by far and away the most common argument supporting theism in the eighteenth century. It rested on the alleged similarity between the world and an elaborately contrived machine and it was just this analogy that Hume attacked, maintaining that there was as much reason, if not more, considering the rise of the biological sciences, for saying that the world resembled not something mechanical as something organic, such as a vegetable. Now we do not observe vegetables coming into existence by the agency of vegetable makers. Why, if we look at the world as an organism, should we assume, therefore, that it requires a maker? If, however, the mechanical model is pressed, Hume argues that it would be more appropriate to postulate a team or a committee of designers and thus arrive at polytheism rather than monotheism. His own explanation of what order there is in the universe is along Epicurean lines, arguing in the manner of Diderot that given infinite time the present world order must emerge; something that was to receive added support in the next century from the Darwinian hypothesis. Hume also pointed to the fact of evil in the world—to what is known as disteleology—as telling against the hypothesis of an intelligent and loving Designer.

With regard to miracles, Hume's argument against their having occurred derives once more from his empiricism, for the argument hinges upon the question of belief in the truth or accuracy of 'testimony'. As is the case with all beliefs which claim to be informative about the world, the belief in miracles must rest on experience, in this instance that men have memories that are usually veracious. But testimonies may conflict and when the 'facts' testified to are marvellous and not corroborated by our own experience of the way in which things happen in the world, then the very same principle of experience which gives us a certain degree of assurance in the testimony of witnesses gives us also, in this case, another degree of assurance against the facts which it seeks to establish. If the event be not only marvellous but miraculous and so violates the established laws of nature, 'as firm and unalterable experience has established those laws', we are confronted by proof against proof and the stronger must prevail. No miraculous event, Hume argues, is so firmly established that it can overthrow the more firmly, because universally, established belief in the laws of nature; no miraculous event so well evidenced that its falsehood would be more miraculous than the 'fact' related.

The ending of the 'Essay on Miracles' is of special interest in that it shows Hume, in the words of Willey, 'delicately poised upon the escarpment of eighteenth century thought, and needing only a touch to topple him down the Kantian incline. Nature is a habit of the mind, morality is a sentiment of the heart, belief is a product of the imagination not of the reason: What next? Hume has accepted all these conclusions, preferring nature to reason in the last resort; will he now tell us that religion is founded on faith not upon reason and urge us to render unto faith that which is faith's?'[20] This, as we have already seen, is just what he does do. In the 'Essay on Miracles' he puts it like this. 'I am the better pleased with the method of reasoning here delivered, as I think it may serve to confound those dangerous friends or disguised enemies to the Christian religion who have undertaken to defend it by the principles of human reason. Our most holy religion is founded on Faith, not on reason, and it is a sure method of exposing it to put it to such a trial as it is by no means fitted to endure.'[21]

It would be tempting to see Hume here embarking upon the same programme that Kant was later to embark upon; as, in Kant's famous words, 'denying reason that he might make room for faith'. This is not, however, what Hume is doing, for it is all too evident elsewhere in his work that the moment sceptical doubt is forgotten and reliance on 'custom' and 'experience' seems to point towards mystery, he falls back on the much depised reason. Beliefs are not reasoning, yet our beliefs must be reasonable. Hume is a child of the Enlightenment in a way that Kant writing at the close of the period never was. Hume's 'faith', we feel, has no depth. It is to be conformed to but in no real way acted upon. Kant, however, will pick up the trend of Hume's work and develop it in a more theistic direction. The critical side of Kant's work however, is as, if not more, formidable than Hume and to that we should now turn.

Kant, like Hume, sets out to destroy the rational basis of eighteenth century theism. Not, however, in the name of atheism or reverent or irreverent agnosticism, but in order that he might establish theism on more solid foundations, immune from the critique of reason. His primary task in the first of his three Critiques—*The Critique of Pure Reason*—is to set out the limits of pure reason and one of his conclusions is that pure reason can tell us nothing whatever about God and any relationship that he might have to the world. His argument is briefly as follows.

He held that we can have no certain knowledge of things-in-themselves, for our experience—in Kant's tortuous terminology 'the transcendental unity of apperception'—is so structured by the constitution of our minds, that we cannot but experience the world as we do. Our minds do not discover a necessary order which is inherent in nature; rather they impose such order upon it. We thus perceive reality as it were through the lenses of our minds. Causality, for example, is just one of the categories by which our minds order reality in space and time—the primary intuitions. This is Kant's answer to Hume and his explanation of the synthetic yet *a priori* character of laws such as those of cause and effect. Thus the Cosmological Argument which asserts that since every event must have a cause and that therefore the world

E

must have a cause, falls to the ground—for necessity attaches to no constraining principle in the world of nature but only to the way in which the mind orders natural phenomena.

There is, moreover, a yet more serious difficulty and one which vitiates any and every attempt to argue from the world to that which lies beyond it; and it is this. The data upon which the mind, by means of the categories, imposes order, originates with phenomena in space and time. Now the Cosmological Argument and the Argument from Design both seek to infer from our experience in space and time to a point outside it—to a transcendent cause. It is precisely this attempt, to move to a point outside all possible experience and observation by means of categories, whose proper and only sphere of application is within space and time, that creates what Kant calls the 'antinomies', or contradictions of pure reason, and so invalidates the argument. How, asks Kant, can we use language derived from and only applicable to our experience within the world to talk meaningfully about either the world conceived as a whole, or about that which lies beyond the world?

If we add Kant's criticism to that of Hume it is understandable why many philosophers today hold that these two thinkers have so undermined the traditional arguments for God's existence as to nullify once and for all the whole programme of natural theology. This has not, however, stopped other philosophers from seeking to restructure the arguments so as to bypass Hume and Kant's critique. Historically, however, the criticism of these two philosophers had an immense and immediate influence; so much so that many in the nineteenth century, and many today, have lost all confidence in the power of speculative reason to make out a case for theistic belief.

Unlike Hume, however, Kant sought to re-establish theism on more solid foundations, and while with Hume, he was prepared to talk about 'faith', he was not prepared to leave that concept unanalysed. What he sought to do was to establish faith in God as a necessary postulate of the moral life—of the life lived according to practical reason. It will be necessary to say something about this in order that we might better understand the atheism of the next century.

Let us begin by noting that Kant was no mere mechanico materialist. He was far too impressed by man's capacity for moral existence to be attracted to a thesis which must deny man's freedom *in toto*. At the phenomenal level of our experience and understanding of nature man might well appear, indeed must appear, a determined being. But this for Kant simply showed the limitations of the phenomenal. Man, he claimed, belonged also to the noumenal world—of things as they were in themselves undetermined by the categories—and knew of that world in moral experience, where he apprehended duty as a categorical imperative wholly unrelated to desire or inclination. Such an imperative was absolute and unconditional. To recognize such an imperative as the basis of the moral life it is necessary, Kant argues, to recognize: Firstly that man has freewill and is not, therefore, determined, as he would be if the mechanico-materialist thesis were true and man wholly part of nature. This he expressed by arguing that the fact that I know that I ought to do $x$ implies that I can do $x$. Secondly I must recognize that I am immortal, since if I am not, then the moral life which sets before me an ideal which it is impossible for me to realize in this life—namely the task of conforming my will to the wholly good will disclosed in the categorical imperative—would be absurd. And lastly, I must recognize the existence of God, who will ultimately bring about the correlation, which is all too evidently not the case in this life, of virtue with happiness.

Man thus lives, for Kant, simultaneously in two spheres: the phenomenal, which is the order of nature as understood by the categories of the understanding, and the noumenal, which is the order of freedom and in which man is aware of the imperatives of the moral life. Because of this dual existence man cannot but be curious concerning the relationship between the two. Does the one aid the other or is the world of phenomena and the phenomenal aspects of man's own being indifferent to his moral striving? Kant believed that questions like these must lead anyone who takes the moral life with utter seriousness to regard nature as the creation of a God who is concerned with moral progress and fulfilment.

It is with such a theism as this and with the corresponding account of morality that many of the atheists of the nineteenth century will wrestle.

So we come to the end of our survey of the atheism of the Enlightenment and some of the issues between belief and unbelief are now, I think, becoming plain. The new science of nature, now firmly established and destined to go triumphantly on its way, has, as articulated by the philosophers, destroyed once and for all the necessity of accounting for the way in which the world works by means of the theistic hypothesis. It has also dispensed with the category of revelation—at least as traditionally correlated with miraculous events. It has further consolidated the tendencies, which we observed as early as the close of the Middle Ages, to restrict the term knowledge to the natural sphere as understood by means of scientific method—a position given near definitive articulation by Kant. The task, therefore, which confronts theism at the end of the eighteenth century is to establish belief, not, as has been shown to be disastrous, on the shifting sand of reasons drawn from the natural world, but on some other basis. Kant shows the way. Others will follow and will seek to establish belief in God not only on moral but also on religious experience. It will occur to few to challenge, before our own day, the whole course of the development of the naturalistic way of looking at the world as the only way of looking at it and the attenuated conception of reason with which it works. For metaphysics it is a time of failure of nerve.

## NOTES

1 *Op cit* p 135

2 Cf especially p 45ff

3 D. Cairns, *Unbelief in the Eighteenth Century* Chapt II on the seventeenth century, p 42

4 Hazard, *European Thought in the Eighteenth Century* p 8

5 B. Willey, *The Eighteenth Century Background* p 47

6 Norman Hampson, Pelican *History of European Thought*, Vol 4, *The Enlightenment* p 75.

7 Cf above p 85–6

8 *Op cit* p 84

9 *Op cit* p 85

10 Hazard, *European Thought in the Eighteenth Century* pp 407–8

11 Burton's *Life of Hume* Vol II, p 220

12 This anyway in the early part of *The System of Nature*. Towards the end there is the lyrical conclusion which so impressed Shelley and which shows that he had not completely rid himself of all religious feeling.

13 I. T. Ramsey, *Religious Language* p 38

14 D'Holbach, *Good Sense* (1772) Chapts CLXVII and CLXVIII. Quoted Margaret Knight, *Humanist Anthology* p 46.

15 It might be worth noting that Patrick Nowell-Smith explains the crimes committed in the name of religion in the following way. He writes: 'And in practice, the objectivist (in ethics) is, as we should expect, in a far worse position for solving moral conflicts. He necessarily attributes his opponents' denial of the truth to wilful perversity; holding as he does that in spite of his denials his opponent must really see the truth all the time, he realizes that what his opponent needs is not argument but castigation . . . the objective theory, so far from minimizing the use of force to settle moral arguments, can be and constantly has been used to justify it. It is no accident that religious persecutions are the monopoly of objective theorists.' *Ethics* pp 46–7

16 Cf A. J. Ayer, *Language, Truth and Logic* p 31, and Gilbert Ryle (Ed) *The Revolution in Philosophy*, Passim.

17 N. Kemp Smith, Introduction to his edition of Hume's *Dialogues Concerning Natural Religion*.

18 Quoted D. Cairns, *Unbelief in the Eighteenth Century* p 91

19 Cf for instance Fr Copleston's formulation in terms of 'explanation' put forward during his exegesis of St Thomas' Five Ways. Copleston, *Aquinas* pp 110ff.

20 Willey, *The Eighteenth Century Background* p 126

21 Hume, *Enquiry Concerning Human Understanding*, Sect X, Pt 11, Selby-Bigge ed Sect 100

# NINE

# THE NINETEENTH CENTURY TO THE PRESENT DAY

KANT'S DETERMINATION to look at moral experience as that which distinguishes man and saves him from complete absorption into the natural sphere is indicative of a growing revulsion from the application of materialistic and mechanical approaches to human life. The man of feeling is beginning to emerge and the dominating movement of the early nineteenth century, which will seek to redress the balance inherited from the Enlightenment, is what is known as the Romantic movement.

But we are now moving towards a more complex, pluralistic era of intellectual history where the unity which has, by and large, characterized the *Zeitgeist* of past periods disappears Thus while Romanticism in the nineteenth century is an important and influential factor, it by no means touches all aspects of the intellectual life of that century and we shall have to look at other movements and individuals that arise and take part in the debate of belief with unbelief. But to turn to the Romantic reaction first.

The Romantic movement admired above all things sensibility. It was also a movement of the individual over against the mass. It is not, therefore, surprising that its foremost religious representative, Friedrich Schleiermacher (1768–1834), should develop a religious apologetic based upon individual religious feeling. It is unfortunate for religion, however, that, as is the case with the Romantic movement generally, with the possible exception of Coleridge, the epistemological prerequisites of such an approach through feeling were never submitted to rigorous philosophical examination. As subsequent criticism was to show, the critical problems posed by such an approach to knowledge about the world—particularly when linked, as it was later to be, to a theology of encounter—were many and they are still with us.

Schleiermacher's theological programme began hopefully. It was, in the words of Rudolf Otto, designed 'to lead an age weary with and alien to religion back to its very mainsprings'.[1] Thus God, for Schleiermacher, is to be found not at the end of a process of natural reasoning, but as the object of the religious consciousness. In an age which valued experience this would appear to be the right beginning. Lacking an articulated epistemology of feeling, however, which would justify 'feeling' as a cognitive activity—as the experience of something—Schleiermacher's attempt to base religion on religious feelings, and particularly on feelings of absolute dependence, was open at the outset to the same criticism that was to dog Kant's attempt to base theism on the dictates of the moral consciousness; namely, that should a naturalistic account of that consciousness be found or some other equally plausible account be given, then theism could be dispensed with. In the same way Schleiermacher's attempt to base theism on the religious consciousness was open to the criticism that it confined God within the religious consciousness, and that it was not inconceivable that that consciousness could be given a naturalistic and non-religious interpretation, and theology transformed into anthropology. This is in fact what happened. For it was just this conclusion that Ludwig Feuerbach (1804–72) drew in his epoch-making work, *The Essence of Christianity* (1841)—which was to have a decisive influence on Karl Marx.

In this work Feuerbach's explicit intention was to turn 'theology into anthropology', 'the science of God into the science of man'. Man's religious consciousness was, for him, simply the projection of man's sublimest ideals onto a supernatural being. Their proper field of application, Feuerbach held, was to man himself—or at least to what man might become. 'God,' as Feuerbach says in another of his works, 'as the epitome of all realities or perfections is nothing other than a compendious summary devised for the benefit of the limited individual, an epitome of the generic human qualities distributed among men, in the self-realization of the species in the course of world history.'[2]

Atheist though he was, however, Feuerbach's aim was not to destroy religion, but, as Engels was later to point out, to perfect it. In Marx's words, Feuerbach's achievement consisted in 'the dissolution of the religious world into its secular basis'.[3] The theistic question Feuerbach regarded as settled. 'The question as to the existence or non-existence of God, the opposition between theism and atheism,' he wrote, 'belongs to the sixteenth and seventeenth centuries, but not to the nineteenth. I deny God. But that means that for me I deny the negation of man.'[4] God must die that man might live. This is the cry that was to be taken up by both Karl Marx (1818–83) and Friedrich Nietzsche (1844–1900).

Marx's way with religion was essentially that of Feuerbach —that is, to reinterpret it. Religion was too significant a phenomenon to be lightly and summarily dismissed. For Marx it represented man's attempt to overcome what he termed 'alienation', and to truly fulfil himself—albeit in a fantastic fashion. He wrote 'The basis of irreligious criticism is: Man makes religion, religion does not make man. In other words, religion is the self-consciousness and self-feeling of man who has either not yet found himself or has already lost himself again. But man is no abstract being squatting outside the world. Man is the world of man, the state, society. This state, this society produce religion, a reversed world-consciousness, because they are a reversed world. Religion is the general theory of that world, its encyclopaedic compendium, its logic in a popular form, its spiritualistic *point d'honneur*, its enthusiasm, its moral sanction, its solemn completion, its universal ground for consolation and justification. It is the fantastic realization of the human essence because the human essence has no true reality. The struggle against religion is therefore mediately the fight against the other world, of which religion is the spiritual aroma.

'Religious distress is at the same time the expression of real distress. Religion is the sigh of the oppressed creature, the heart of a heartless world, just as it is the spirit of a spiritless situation. It is the opium of the people.

'The abolition of religion as the illusory happiness of the people is required for their real happiness. The demand to give up the illusions about its condition is the demand to give up a condition which needs illusions.'[5]

But while religion is relegated to the realm of fantasy, it represented for Marx something significant in human life, something that indicated that society must be changed in order that a more real and truly human fulfilment might be achieved. Marx's analysis and understanding of religion has a depth which many of the more superficial attempts to get at the origins and persistence of religion do not possess, although Marx himself toyed with some of these—such as for instance that religion simply arose out of man's fear of nature —at other times in his life. The account Marx offers brings him close to Freud (1856–1939) who also relegated religion to the world of fantasy-fulfilment. But before turning to Freud we must first look at that other great nineteenth century atheist Friedrich Nietzsche.

Nietzsche is one of the seminal minds of the modern European consciousness, its profoundest psychologist and its most accurate prophet. He himself characterizes the situation from which his thinking began by giving it the name of 'nihilism'. This was the feature of the latter part of the nineteenth century which he saw as a challenge which had to be faced. That he did so is somewhat remarkable. For consider the historical situation at the time at which he was writing. Prussian arms had established German supremacy on the Continent. Britain was conscious of her supremacy at sea. Science and technology were beginning to make spectacular and hitherto unheard of advances. Reform was rife and optimism was common. Yet, for Nietzsche, the political stability and the material improvements of the age were as nothing compared with the one fact which for him mattered, but to which the eyes and ears of his contemporaries were blind and deaf. God was dead.

In the *Gay Science*, published in 1882, we find this parable. 'Have you ever heard of the madman who on a bright morning lit a lantern and ran to the market place and cried out unceasingly, "I seek God, I seek God!"? As many of those who heard him did not believe in God were standing around, he provoked much laughter. "Why, is he lost?" said one. "Did he lose his way like a child?" said another. "Or is he hiding?" . . . thus they yelled and laughed. The madman jumped into their midst and transfixed them with his glances. "Whither is God?" he cried. "I shall tell you. We have killed him—you and I. All of us are his murderers. But how have we done this? How were we able to drink up the sea? Who gave us the sponge to wipe away the entire horizon? What did we do when we unchained this earth from its sun? Whither is it moving now? Whither are we moving now? Away from all suns? Are we not plunging continually? Backward, sideward, forward, in all directions? Is there any up or down left? Are we not straying as through infinite nothingness? Do we not feel the breath of empty space? Has it not become colder? Is not night and more night coming on all the while? . . . God is dead. God remains dead. And we have killed him. What was holiest and most powerful of all the world has yet owned has bled to death under our knives. Who will wipe this blood off us? Is not the magnitude of this deed too great for us? Shall we not ourselves have to become gods, merely to seem worthy of it?" . . . Here the madman fell silent and looked again at his hearers, and they too were silent and looked at him in astonishment. At last he threw his lantern on the ground and it broke and went out. "I come too early" he said. "My time has not yet come". "This tremendous event is still on its way . . . it has not yet reached the ears of man. Lightning and thunder require time, the light of the stars requires time, deeds require time even after they are done before they can be seen and heard. This deed is still more distant from them than the most distant stars—and yet they have done it themselves." It is further stated that the madman made his way into different churches and there sang his *Requiem aeternam deo*. When led out and called to account he always gave the same reply: "What are these churches now, if they are not the tombs and monuments of God".'[6]

We have lost our faith in God, says Nietzsche, and with more acumen than the majority of late nineteenth century intellectuals, especially those in England, Nietzsche spells out the consequences of this, particularly in the realm of values. There remains, he says, only the void. Our dignity is gone; our traditional values are in confusion and who can say any longer what is up and what is down. With the ancient Hebrew prophets Nietzsche had that capacity and ability to experience his own wretched fate so deeply that it became the allegory of something larger. He felt the agony, the suffering and the misery of what it was to live in a godless world so deeply, at a time when the majority of his contemporaries were wholly insensitive to the consequences of unbelief, that he was able to experience in advance the fate of a coming generation.

Nietzsche's philosophy, however, is not one of fatalistic despair. It is a positive attempt to restructure our whole value system on foundations other than those of traditional theism. Nietzche's task is to substitute for a transcendental morality deriving its *raison d'être* from the will of God and a divinely orientated teleology a naturalistic morality deriving its *raison d'être* from the human condition. 'If God be dead' exclaims Ivan Karamazov in Dostoievsky's novel, *The Brothers Karamazov*, 'all is permitted.' Yet whereas the recognition of this bewilders Ivan and drives him to despair, in Nietzsche it becomes a cry of triumphant affirmation. From the proclamation of the death of God Nietzsche is led to call for a 'transvaluation of all values' and for a new breed of men, the 'overmen' (*übermensch*)—often but wrongly translated supermen—who will overcome man as he now is and be able to live with and exemplify in their lives man's newly discovered sense of dreadful freedom.

He is also led in the *Genealogy of Morals* as well as in *The Anti-Christ*, two of his later works, to what, as he himself recognized, was the first full scale attack on Christian moral values.

How different the reaction of English intellectuals as expressed in a note made by Sir Leslie Stephen in 1856 when he had lost his religious faith. 'I now believe in nothing,' he wrote, '. . . but I do not the less believe in morality etc, etc. I mean to live and die like a gentleman if possible.'[7] As Quentin Bell has commented: 'The implication is clear; Stephen might consider that the Christian views concerning the origin and ultimate destiny of men and women were false; but in practice this in no way changed his opinions concerning honourable conduct.'[8]

Dr Bronowski makes a similar point. Writing of the fear on the part of Orthodoxy that unbelief would lead to a breakdown of traditional morality he characterizes the reply of the unbelievers as follows: 'No, replied Huxley and John Stuart Mill and George Eliot and Bagehot; we are plainly all people of the highest rectitude; and therefore the moral sense must be inborn in every man.'[9] One consequence of this, as Bronowski further points out, was that they felt personally bound to live lives of quite monumental dullness even when they sinned.[10]

Religious scepticism on the one hand, moral orthodoxy on the other. This was not a combination destined to survive the test of time, for the breakdown of the hitherto religious and teleogically orientated outlook on life was fraught as Nietzsche saw with the most far reaching consequences for morality. It was to be left to our own generation to draw the conclusions. To a large extent this is the burden of the message put forward today by the Existentialists, in which nineteenth century Romantic atheism comes to fulfilment.

## Atheistic Existentialism

Not all existentialists are, of course, atheists. Many, such as Marcel, a Catholic, and Buber, a Jew, are theists. Jaspers and Heidegger would I think describe themselves as reverent agnostics. But in the movement associated with the name of Jean-Paul Sartre, (1905–), which for many is identical with existentialism, atheism is taken for granted. It is indeed the first premise. 'If God be dead, all is permitted. That' says Sartre, 'is existentialism's starting point.'[11] And his main concern is to work out the conclusions for morality of a consistently held atheistic position. For Sartre, as for most existentialists, the problem of God is real, and not, as for so many Anglo-Saxon philosophers today, a pseudo one. To raise the question of God is, for him, to raise the question of the meaning of human life. If there is no God then there is no meaning written into human life. God and teleology are inextricably linked together. The question of God's existence having been answered in the negative,[12] meaning must be supplied by each individual for himself.

Albert Camus (1913–60) also wrestled with the same problem in his book, *The Myth of Sisyphus*. Life, for Camus, was at bottom 'absurd'—a concept which for him arose at that point where man's desire for meaning met the blank indifference of the universe. Camus, however, goes beyond the despair that characterized Sartre's early existentialism and he seeks to offer a positive solution to the problem of living in an absurd, because godless, universe which will be valid and relevant for all.

To explore the response of other creative writers to the breakdown of the theistic world view would take us far beyond the modest task which we have set ourselves in this work, but it is worth noting that it has provided one of the major themes of the literature of our century, an indication of the seriousness, in the realm of feeling at least, of the crisis through which our civilization and its culture is passing.

## Science and Religion

Returning to the nineteenth century one major strand in unbelief which now comes firmly to the centre of the picture is the scientific criticism. To attempt to deal at all adequately with this in relation to the nineteenth century would require another book. The most that we can do here is to instance some of the more important aspects, particularly as these illustrate the growing tendency to interpret religion and religious experience naturalistically. We must also note that the earlier mechanico-materialist criticism now becomes part of the popular criticism of religion and has remained so to our own day.

To begin with Freud (1856–1939), who, despite his having initiated one of the major scientific advances of the twentieth century, is philosophically very much of a nineteenth century turn of mind. With Marx and Nietzsche, Freud argues that a morality based upon religious premises is suspect. Man must learn in this as in other fields to stand upon his own two feet. But whereas, as we have seen, Marx pinned his hopes of a new morality on a renewal of society and Nietzsche on a new disciplined and self-sufficient breed of men, Freud's hope rests on science. Again, with Marx and Nietzsche, Freud has also made up his mind, in advance of what he has to say about religion, that religious claims about the world are invalid.[13] He, therefore, seeks simply to account for the empirical phenomenon of religion in naturalistic terms.

As G. S. Spinks has pointed out, all of Freud's writings on

religion, and there are many, are for the most part variations on the theme of God as the 'magnified father'.[14] Theism, for Freud, is basically the outcome of what he calls 'projection'— the projection on to the universe at large of what are, in fact, only psychological processes. This comes out clearly in his book, *The Future of an Illusion* (1927). Culture, argues Freud, requires the renunciation of our most primitive instincts; but such renunciation will only be possible if some substitute gratification is found. Of all substitute gratifications the most widespread has been religion. But religious belief is declining —is being increasingly seen to be an illusion—and Freud's fear is that unless other more stable substitute gratifications are found then civilization and culture will collapse. His sense of doom is almost as great as Nietzsche's. But this is not our concern here. What we are concerned with is why it was that Freud thought that those who regarded religion as an illusion were right. His case is both philosophical and psychological. Philosophically, Freud accepted the scientific and anti-religious presuppositions of his day. 'The riddles of the universe' he writes, 'only reveal themselves slowly to our enquiry, to many questions science can as yet give no answer; but scientific work is our only way to knowledge of reality.'[15] Theism, he holds, cannot be established by such methods and it is therefore to be dismissed, though Freud never really gets down to a close consideration of the philosophical basis of theism and he never really goes into the actual reasons for his philosophical rejection of religion. He tells us himself, in his autobiography, that he had little taste for philosophy. 'Even when I have moved away from observation,' he tells us, 'I have carefully avoided any contact with philosophy proper. This avoidance has been greatly facilitated by constitutional incapacity.'[16]

His case against religion is therefore on the surface primarily psychological. Religion is a form of wish-fulfilment. Life is hard to endure, and Man seeks comfort from life's harsh realities by personifying the impersonal forces of nature and, in attempting to bribe them, obtains some relief. The proto-type of this situation is the helplessness of childhood, where comfort is sought in the parent. Religion, and particularly theism, is therefore, for Freud, a regression back to childhood. The religious man, helpless and afraid before the universe, projects on to nature the comforting figure of the father and thus creates his god.

This explanation of the origin of religion would not, of course, of itself show that the religious man was mistaken, and Freud is careful to distinguish 'illusion' from 'error'. An 'illusion' is derived from man's wishes. It is wish-fulfilment. That it is also an error must be established independently. Religion for Freud was both illusion and error—an illusion because it was a wish-fulfilment, and error because, as we have seen, Freud believed that it could not be independently estab-lished on rational and scientific grounds. This latter, therefore, is the strength of Freud's case, as it had been the strength of the case against religion almost from Freud's childhood. In the nineteenth century it might almost be called the standard argument against religion. We have seen its beginnings. We must now look at the developments of the scientific criticism in the second half of the nineteenth century. And it was in England that the debate between science and religion was conducted in real earnest. Much of it is concerned with argu-ments against specific Christian doctrines, such as the date and manner of creation, rather than with theism as such. This is for the most part the case with regard to Darwinism—the *cause célèbre* of the time—which challenged traditional Chris-tian assumptions concerning the origin of man as this was derived from the Hebraic scriptures. Darwin's theory of natural selection, put forward in his epoch-making work, *The Origin of Species* (1859), did, however, challenge theism as such in that it cast doubt upon the traditional argument from design, offering a naturalistic account of the internal coherence of animal bodies and of their adaptation to environment. According to Darwin's theory animals are relatively efficient organisms in relation to their environment for the simple reason that less well adapted individuals have perished in the continual competiton to survive and so have not perpetuated their kind. The struggle for survival operating as a constant pressure towards perfect adaptation lies behind the evolution of life into ever increasingly complex forms.

Darwin himself (1809–82), was, in fact, an agnostic about the effect of his theory on the argument from design, alternating between being impressed on the one hand by evolutionary development and on the other becoming oppressed by the facts of disteleology. 'There seems to me,' he wrote in one of his letters, 'too much misery in the world. I cannot persuade myself that a beneficent and omnipotent God would have designedly created the *Ichneumonidae* with the express intention of their feeding within the living bodies of caterpillars or that a cat should play with mice. Not believing this, I see no necessity in the belief that the eye was expressly designed. On the other hand, I cannot anyhow be contented to view this wonderful universe, and especially the nature of man, and to conclude that everything is the result of brute force. I am inclined to look at everything as resulting from designed laws, with the details, whether good or bad, left to the working out of what we may call chance. Not that this notion at all satisfies me. I feel most deeply that the whole subject is too profound for the human intellect . . . Let each man hope and believe what he can.'[17]

The evolutionary hypothesis turned out to be more far reaching in its implications for religion than the Darwinian controversy suggests, for it was part of a wider historical sense which in the opinion of many is the nineteenth century's chief contribution to intellectual history. For the first time religion began to be studied historically and comparatively and this could not but call into question any and every doctrine which claimed to be definitive. As Noël Annan puts it, 'Men began to see Truth no longer as absolute, philosophically static, revealed once and for all, but as relative, genetic and evolutionary.'[18]

It was in the eighteen-seventies that the debate between science and religion began in earnest. The spark which began it was struck in Oxford during the well-known debate concerning the descent of man between Thomas Huxley and Bishop Wilberforce which took place at a meeting of the British Association for the Advancement of Science in 1860. Until that time the 'rationalists' as they gained some advantage by calling themselves, had for the most part, held their fire. But after the Oxford squabble the moral fervour passed into the hands of the Agnostics—as they were now to call themselves.[19] As Noël Annan explains, 'By the seventies a group of men, Huxley, Leslie Stephen, John Morley and the brilliant young geometer W. K. Clifford, set about converting the public in the periodicals with an Evangelical zest.'[20] Scientific Humanism as a popular creed was launched. A contemporary apostle has defined it thus: 'To describe someone as a Humanist' writes Margaret Knight, 'implies that he sees no reason for believing in a supernatural God, or in a life after death; that he holds that man must face his problems with his own intellectual and moral resources, without evoking supernatural aid; and that authority, supernatural or otherwise, should not be allowed to obstruct enquiry in any field of thought.'[21]

With these basic beliefs there go two common corollaries. 'First, that virtue is a matter of promoting human well being . . . and secondly, that the mainsprings of moral action are . . . the social instincts.'[21]

Two humanists merit our special attention, John Stuart Mill (1806–73) and Bertrand Russell (1872–1970), Mill's godson—though, as Mill insisted when accepting the honour, 'in the purely secular sense'.

In his *Autobiography* Mill describes himself as 'one of the very few examples in this country, of one who has not thrown off religious belief, but never had it'.[22] But like his father, James Mill, who had once been a candidate for Holy Orders, John Stuart continued to take religion seriously, and thought its claims worthy of serious refutation. In his *Three Essays on Religion*, written towards the end of his life, Mill makes a sustained attempt to go over once again the arguments for and against belief in God. His conclusions were almost entirely negative, and his prime objection is a moral one. Looking out on the suffering in the world Mill found it morally repugnant to believe that such a world as ours is could be the loving creating of a perfectly good and all powerful deity.

In his own memorable words: 'If the law of all creation were justice and the creator omnipotent, then, in whatever amount suffering and happiness might be dispensed to the world, each person's share of them would be exactly proportioned to that person's good or evil deeds. . . . No one is able to blind himself to the fact that the world we live in is totally different from this, insomuch that the necessity for redressing the balance has been deemed one of the strongest arguments for another life after death, which amounts to an admission that the order of things in this life is often an example of injustice, not justice. If it be said that God does not take sufficient account of pleasure and pain to make them the reward or punishment of the good and the wicked, but that virtue itself is the greatest good and vice the greatest evil, then these at least ought to be dispensed to all according to what they have done to deserve them; instead of which every kind of moral depravity is entailed upon the multitude by the fatality of their birth, through the fault of their parents, of society, or of uncontrollable circumstances, certainly through no fault of their own. Not even the most distorted and contracted theory of good which was ever framed by religion or philosophical fanaticism can the government of nature be made to resemble the work of a being at once good and omnipotent.'[23]

On another occasion his repugnance reaches the heights of Promethean defiance. 'I will call no Being good,' he says, 'who is not what I mean when I apply that epithet to my fellow creatures; and if such a Being can sentence me to Hell for not so calling Him, to Hell I will go.'

For Mill, as for so many others, then and now, the facts in the world which when brought into relationship with theistic belief in an all-good and all-powerful creator give rise to the problem of evil tell convincingly against such a belief.

Russell's atheism is classic not to say monumental. It is also founded upon nineteenth century premises. For Russell the universe is a brute fact. It just is.[24] Science adequately explains, or eventually will explain, its workings, and nothing more needs to be said. Only once, in an essay entitled, 'A Free Man's Worship',[25] did Russell permit himself to detract from this attitude and to rail, Mill-like, at the universe for being other than he would wish it to be.

## Logical Positivism and Logical Empiricism

The criticism of religion from the standpoint of science has been made more precise in our own day by being formulated in terms derived from the current interest in semantics and the philosophy of language. This can be seen in the criticism of religious language as meaningless put forward during the first part of the century by the movement known as Logical Positivism, of which the now Wyckam Professor of Logic at Oxford, Professor Sir A. J. Ayer, was the most vociferous exponent. The movement originated, however, in Vienna.

Taking scientific language as the model for all meaningful language about the world, the Positivists answered the question as to what made scientific language meaningful by putting forward a criterion of meaning known as the 'verification principle'. This was variously formulated, but essentially it was maintained that (*a*) for a proposition to be meaningful we should know in principle at least how it might be verified (or falsified), and (*b*) that only sense-verification counted as verification. Religious (as well as ethical and aesthetic) propositions were, it was claimed, unable to meet this requirement and were therefore dismissed as nonsensical.

A clear and unequivocal statement of this position can be found in chapter six of Ayer's justly renowned *Language, Truth and Logic* (1936). For Ayer there are two types of meaningful propositions. There are, on the one hand, analytic propositions—what are better known as tautologies—which tell us nothing about the world but simply record our determination to use symbols in a certain way. Such are definitions and the whole of mathematics and logic. On the other hand there are synthetic or empirical propositions which do tell us something about the world. The criterion of meaning for these latter is the verification principle. Religious propositions falling into neither class are reduced to some other more amenable because more empirical form of statement or dismissed altogether as meaningless.

Of this attack on religion Professor J. J. C. Smart of Adelaide University wrote: 'The greatest danger to theism at the present moment does not come from the people who deny the validity of the arguments for the existence of God, for many Christian theologians do not believe that the existence of God can be proved. . . . The main danger to theism comes from the people who want to say that "God exists" and "God does not exist" are equally absurd. The concept of God they would say is a nonsensical one.'[26]

In similar vein Professor John Mcquarrie warned religious men that 'the challenge which linguistic philosophy offers to theological thinking is one which will have to be faced', and he pointed out that 'it is one of the most radical challenges ever offered to theology, since it concerns not simply the truth but the very meaning of religious statements'.[27] Ayer and those who followed him had certainly struck home.

In the history of atheism this position is somewhat unique—

although, as we have seen in the first part of this study, it is a position that to some extent was anticipated by Carneades' criticism of the Stoic conception of God. It is perhaps worth stating it in Ayer's own words. In the last resort Ayer is neither theist, nor atheist, nor agnostic. As he himself says: 'It is important not to confuse this view of religious assertions with the view that is adopted by atheists and agnostics. For it is a characteristic of an agnostic to hold that the existence of a god is a possibility in which there is no good reason either to believe or disbelieve; and it is characteristic of an atheist to hold that it is at least probable that no god exists. And our view that all utterances about the nature of God are nonsensical, so far from lending support to either of these familiar contentions, is actually incompatible with them. For if the assertion that there is a god is nonsensical, then the atheist's assertion that there is no god is equally nonsensical, since it is only a significant proposition that can be significantly contradicted. As for the agnostic, although he refrains from saying either that there is or is not a god, he does not deny that the question whether a transcendent god exists is a genuine question. He does not deny that the two sentences 'There is a transcendent god' and 'There is no transcendent god' express propositions one of which is actually true and the other false. All he says is that we have no means of telling which of them is true, and therefore ought not to commit ourselves to either. But we have seen that the sentences in question do not express propositions at all. And this means that agnosticism also is ruled out.'[28]

Ayer wrote that in 1936. Today the situation has changed but I would not myself say that it has fundamentally altered. Under the influence of the later writings of Wittgenstein—published posthumously, often on the basis of notes taken at his lectures by pupils—philosophers today are more aware than ever before of the complex functions of language, or of what Wittgenstein himself called the variety of logical grammars or language games. The critique of religious language, of its forms and functions, is now seen to be nowhere near so simple a task as Ayer's fifteen-page dismissal would suggest. I would suggest, however, that, aware as we now are of the manifold logic of religious language, the issue which Ayer so clearly and unequivocally stated with reference to the cognitive claims of certain religious propositions to tell us something informative about the world and its relationship to God still remains the central issue theism has to face. It may be, as many theologians and religious philosophers now openly state,[29] that religion is a 'blik',[30] a perspective, an attitude, a way of looking at the world, rather than a descriptive account of how reality actually is. But to take up such a position is not only to abandon the traditional claims of theistic religion, it is to admit that the naturalistic way of understanding and interpreting reality, its methods and its categories, is the only way; and naturalism precludes religion from the cognitive realm. Many theologicans are prepared to take this view. On the other hand many are not and are seeking, like the late Dr A. M. Farrer, Professor E. L. Mascall, Fr Copleston and many others, to develop and extend the old programme of natural theology, convinced that the mind can establish, rationally, knowledge of the being and nature of a transcendent God. Yet others, like the present Bishop of Durham, Dr I. T. Ramsey, are seeking to develop a natural theology based upon a wider empiricism than that which has been operative since about the middle of the seventeenth century. The issue is still open.

## NOTES

1 Rudolf Otto, Introduction to the Harper Torch Books edition of Schleiermacher's *On Religion—Speeches to its Cultured Despisers* pp vii–viii

2 Feuerbach, *The Philosophy of the Future* p 28

3 Marx, *Theses on Feuerbach* IV

4 Feuerbach, *Essence of Christianity* p 26

5 Karl Marx, *Contribution to the Critique of Hegel's Philosophy of Right.* K.

Marx and F. Engels, *On Religion*, (Foreign Languages Publishing House, Moscow) pp 41–43.

[6] F. Nietzsche, *The Gay Science* p 125

[7] Quoted Quentin Bell, *Bloomsbury* p 24

[8] *Ibid*

[9] J. Bronowski, 'Unbelief and Science' in *Ideas and Beliefs of the Victorians*.

[10] *Ibid*

[11] J.-P. Sartre, *Existentialism and Humanism* p 1

[12] Sartre does in fact offer a proof of God's non-existence. Cf *Being and Nothingness* Trans Hazel E. Barnes; Trans Intro pp xxix ff.

[13] Freud according to Ernest Jones was a natural atheist. He writes: 'He grew up devoid of any belief in God or Immortality and does not appear to have felt the need of it.' *Sigmund Freud*, Vol 1, p 22

[14] G. S. Spinks, *Psychology and Religion* p 75

[15] S. Freud, *The Future of an Illusion* p 55

[16] S. Freud, *An Autobiographical Study* p 109

[17] Darwin to Asa Gray. Quoted John Greene, *Darwin and the Modern World View* p 44

[18] Noël Annan, 'Strands of Unbelief' in *Ideas and Beliefs of the Victorians* p 151

[19] The word itself was coined by Huxley to define his own position within the Metaphysical Society founded in 1869 for the serious and respectable discussion of the issues between science and religion.

[20] Noël Annan, *op cit* p 154

[21] Margaret Knight, *Humanist Anthology* p xiii

[22] Mill, *Autobiography*; Essential Works of John Stuart Mill, Bantam Classics Edit p 34

[23] Mill, *Three Essays*, essay 'On Nature'; The Essential Works of John Stuart Mill, Bantam Classics Edit p 386

[24] Cf His remarks about this made in the debate with Fr Copleston; reprinted in his book *Why I am not a Christian*.

[25] Published in Russell, *Mysticism and Logic*.

[26] J. J. C. Smart. 'The Existence of God' in *New Essays in Philosophical Theology*, Ed A. N. G. Flew and A. MacIntyre.

[27] J. Mcquarrie in *Expository Times* Vol LXVIII, No 12, Sept 1957, p 365

[28] A. J. Ayer, *Language, Truth and Logic* pp 115–16

[29] eg R. B. Braithwaite, *An Empiricist's View of the Nature of Religious Belief*, P. Van Buren, *The Secular Meaning of the Gospel*.

[30] Cf R. M. Hare, 'Theology and Falsification' Sect B in *New Essays in Philosophical Theology*, Edit A. G. N. Flew and A. MacIntyre.

# CONCLUSION

This brings me to the end of my survey of Western atheism —from the breakdown of the mythological world view brought about by the Pre-Socratic philosophers of Ancient Greece to the consistent naturalism of our own day. Whether or no a pattern has emerged I will leave to others to judge. Certainly it would appear that the development observed in Classical Antiquity occurs again in Europe from the Renaissance onwards, except that this time the move is away from nature regarded as a living organism, shot through with divinity, towards a conception of nature devoid of life and meaning other than that which can be quantified in the categories of natural science. This development is not yet complete. Man himself remains—unquantified and—and this is the question—unquantifiable? Man as a subject for science is still, as Professor Sir Alfred Ayer shows in a recent paper under that title,[1] still a matter for dispute.

I would suggest, therefore, that the next stage of the debate between belief and unbelief with regard to the existence of God will centre around the being of man and it may well be that those intractable areas of man's own being will provide the analogy by which an attempt will be made to look again at the world and to see whether or no there are areas of man's relationship with and apprehension of the world which are not amenable to scientific method, areas in which he becomes aware of God.

Has man perhaps some other mode of apprehending and understanding the reality which surrounds him that has yet to be articulated?[2] I don't know. Of one thing I am certain, and that is that the full story has not been told and that the debate between those who see the world and understand it naturalistically and those who, however vaguely, feel dissatisfied with this and discern that there is more 'beyond', 'behind' or 'within' nature and the being of man, and which they more often than not call 'God' or the 'Divine', will continue for a long time to come.

NOTES

[1] A. J. Ayer, 'Man as a Subject for Science' in *Philosophy, Politics and Society* Ed Peter Lasslett and W. G. Runciman.

[2] The experimental Research Centre for Religious Experience recently established in Oxford under the direction of Sir Alisdair Hardy points the way here, although it is early days yet to say what, if anything, the results of this venture might prove.

# INDEX OF NAMES

# SUBJECT INDEX